I0475573

Dark Horizons

Dark Horizons

Tales of Supernatural, Suspense, and Mystery

Billy Van

artisanPruett

Dark Horizons

Copyright © 2023 by Billy Van
All rights reserved. No part of this book may be reproduced or transmitted in any form or by any means without written permission of the author.

Typeset in Garamond

ISBN: 978-1-312-69468-2

Edited by: John Stall
Foreword by: John Stall
Cover Art by: Wicked Design
Cover Design by: Artistic Madmen

April 8, 2023

Printed in the United States of America

For Salina

In Memory of Angela Lynch Padgett

Acknowledgments

I would like to thank the following: Salina DeBose and Brittany Marie Van for being my biggest support system, John Stall for editing and writing my foreword, Dark Horizons for supplying me with such great cover art, and Wicked Tree Development for their cover design. Thank you all. And thanks to St. Vincent's in Indianapolis, Indiana for my being here today.

And to Salina and Brittany, I want to take a moment to express my heartfelt gratitude for the unwavering support and love that you have shown me throughout my life.

Salina, you have been my rock, my confidant, and my partner in everything. Your unwavering support and encouragement have kept me going through tough times, and your love and affection have given me the strength to keep pushing forward. I am truly blessed to have you in my life.

Brittany, you are the light of my life, and I am so proud of the person you have become. Your intelligence, compassion, and creativity inspire me every day, and I am grateful for the joy and happiness that you bring into my life.

I want you both to know that I could not have achieved anything without your love, support, and encouragement. You have always been there for me, through thick and thin, and I will always cherish the memories we have made together.

Thank you, Salina and Brittany, for being the most important people in my life. I love you both more than words can express.

With gratitude and love,
B.V.

Foreword

Dear reader,

Welcome to a world where darkness reigns supreme and fear knows no bounds. Within the pages of this collection of horror stories, you will encounter the macabre and the malevolent, the haunting and the horrific. Billy Van, the master of terror, has crafted a series of tales that will grip you with a vice-like hold and refuse to let go.

In Dark Horizons, Billy Van has explored the depths of the human psyche, delving into the darkest recesses of the mind to uncover the horrors that lurk within. With his masterful storytelling and his ability to conjure up a sense of unease and dread, Van has created a collection of stories that will leave you trembling with fear.

The stories in this collection are not for the faint of heart. From the murky depths of the ocean to the depths of the human soul, these stories will take you on a journey into the unknown, into a world where the lines between reality and nightmare are blurred. Be warned, for once you begin reading, there is no turning back. The monsters that lurk within these pages are not the kind that can be easily vanquished. They are the stuff of nightmares, the phantoms that haunt your dreams.

Van's ability to create vivid, unsettling imagery is unparalleled. His prose is so vivid that it will send shivers down your spine. He understands the human psyche and knows how to manipulate it to create truly terrifying stories. Whether it's a tale of demonic possession or a haunting in an abandoned asylum, Van has a talent for crafting stories that will leave you with a sense of foreboding long after you have finished reading.

As you journey through the pages of Dark Horizons, you will encounter a world that is both familiar and yet terrifyingly different. The stories in this collection will take you to places that you never thought possible, introducing you to characters that are both relatable and yet utterly horrifying. You will feel their fear, their pain, and their desperation, as they struggle to survive in a world that is overrun by darkness.

So, brace yourself for a journey into the unknown, into a world where the lines between reality and nightmare are blurred. Welcome to Dark Horizons, where every turn of the page will take you deeper into the abyss of fear.

Yours in terror,
John Stall

Table of Contents

Ghostly

"Things are not always what they seem;
The first appearance deceives many;
The intelligence of a few perceives
What has been carefully hidden."

—*Phaedrus*

I know I've seen her before—her eyes, her smile, even her scent held familiar attributes to my liking. But the question remained—just who was she?—this beautiful creature. I knew what I had to do. If it was the very last thing I did, I had to reel her in. So I studied her from a distance—where she ate, where she shopped, and her daily and nightly routines, therein. But I had to be careful—there was a killer on the loose. He's been laying low for the past week, inadvertently, about the same time I submitted to my subconscious obsession.

"Hi, my name is Will. And you are?"

"My name is Stephanie."

The way she moved:—she fluttered with the wind, like a butterfly ebbing through flickering embers unscathed. Like falling in love with a ghost, I had not met her personally but I was a slave to her clandestine existence—an existence to which only I was in the know.

Alas, I had a problem…a big problem. I was an introvert. A creature of the night, but she cured me. She enabled me to absorb the light—to walk beyond the public and be social. But how could I be social with her? How could I tether our psyche so we could share our thoughts like cerebral whispers? The clever thing would be a simple introduction. But I was anxious—not so much concerned about rejection moreover hearing her delicate voice and falling into a deeper obsession.

This, I imagined, and played *it* over and over in my head:

"Hi, my name is Will. And you are?" I never even knew her name, but for the sake of continuing, I invented one.

"My name is Stephanie."

"Stephanie, such a befitting name," so elegant, yet so simple, "almost as beautiful as you."

Blushing, she replied, "I'm very flattered, Will." She smiled, "You're not too bad yourself." And just like that, she vanished.

I continued to replay our conversation, but it always ended the same. Hence, I mustn't let her out of my sight. I'd catch up with her soon and woo her like a true gentleman.

We made our way through town—over the babbling brook and through the park. I kept my distance whilst dodging behind trees. She would occasionally look back, but I was more than certain I had gone unnoticed.

What seemed like it took a good hour, she finally reached her destination. It was the old Miller's plantation—thought to be abandoned for years. And at that point, I was more curious than anything. Why of all places would she have, unknowingly, lured me here?

I didn't follow her inside—my forethought was prominent with foresight. However, I couldn't resist engaging in a little snooping. I gingerly preyed upon the sound that resonated from inside the empty dilapidating shell. There seemed to be a window at every stop she made as I carefully peeked inside. I should have left well enough alone for what I saw next chilled me to the very core.

There I was, lying in a cold storage bed—dismembered.

She entered the room, walked up to the window, gazed callously in my direction, and said, "Stop haunting me!" I turned around and found myself surrounded by many others like me—unresponsive with empty and glossy, opaque eyes.

Lines of Distinction (Original Draft)

Chapter One

The Present

Dover, IL. Pop. 1800

Jeff Roberts never took anything for granted. In fact, he had it made. He had a nice job—Chief Investigator for the Dover Police Department. And he had a beautiful wife—Linda. And to top things off his partner Dale Wilson was also his best friend.

He and his wife resided in a nice little "two-story" two bedroom house. They dreamed of someday having kids. Well, they were both in their mid-thirties so Mr. Stork had better hurry.

Every Thursday night Jeff and Dale would get together after work and go play pool at Marty's GameRoom. That's how it was spelled—GameRoom—scrunched together with a capital G and capital R.

In the quiet little town of Dover, not a lot happened. The crime rate was extremely low. At that, the only thing the citizens of Dover had any concern about was an old hermit by the name of Curtis Blackwell. However, I'll explain more about him later.

One day, a teenage boy cut himself with a rusty pocketknife and was taken to the ER. It went around the whole town that someone had been shot nearly to death. News circulated fast and usually manifested into a pretense by the time it reached its end.

On this particular night, Dale shared a secret with Jeff. It was strange in a sense and totally caught Jeff off guard. He said, "Jeff, I think of you as a brother. I got something to tell ya." Dale paused for a moment. "I can't shoot a man."

"And you're a cop?"

"Seriously...I just can't!"

"And why not, Dale?"

Dale began to cry. "My brother was shot when he was only six. A stray bullet came out of nowhere."

"You haven't pulled that trigger once since I've known ya. It makes sense now. Hell, does your gun even work? It's probably stuffed full of cobwebs." Jeff laughed and Dale joined in. "You'll be all right, Dale. I'll help you through this."

Jeff ordered two beers. He said, "You owe me," and laughed. Dale knew he was joking. Jeff didn't have to laugh. Dale knew Jeff all too well. Jeff was always acting uptight and saying that people owed him. He meant it all as a joke for he had plenty of money.

One beer turned into two. Two beers turned into three. Three beers turned to whiskey shots—no chaser. It wasn't too long before Jeff awoke the next morning confused at how he had gotten home. And he had the worst hangover he had ever experienced.

Linda made him a pot of coffee.

She irritated the grumpy bear. "Coffee's on—unless you wannanother beer. How about a little hair of the dog this mornin', sunshine?"

Jeff was in no mood for her early morning antics.

He snapped at Linda, which was not like Jeff at all. He tolerated it a lot—not this morning. He took Linda by surprise with his uncouth demeanor.

"You don't have to be such a jerk!" Linda said softly as she turned and walked away.

"Cook my breakfast and shut the hell up," Jeff replied in a gruff tone—almost a growl.

By now Linda was concerned. Jeff never woke up in this mood. She thought to herself: *Later, I will have a talk with Jeff about his drinking.* She would give him an ultimatum. Either he would stay sober or she would leave. At this point either way she would come out even-steven.

Jeff rolled over, grabbed the remote control from off his bedside table, and turned on his hi-def television. He was immediately aware of what was playing. It was a rerun of the two-thousand-eight Dr. Jekyll and Mr. Hyde series. Jeff knew this because he used to watch it when it was actually being aired.

He stared at it for a moment and said, "Not my favorite episode," then, turned off the television.

He crawled out of bed wearing nothing but his boxer shorts and headed for the bathroom. Conveniently they had a bathroom inside their bedroom.

By now Linda was downstairs preparing breakfast.

She was not at all happy with Jeff.

At one point, before he and Linda got married, Jeff was an alcoholic. She agreed to marry him on the condition that he quit his drinking. He loved her so much. As hard as it was for him to turn his back on the bottled beast he did—never to look back. Linda was so afraid that his addiction would hark back into his verve. This would cause superfluous worry on her part.

As Jeff stood in the shower—standing beneath the steady stream of water as if his body was a human waterfall—he began to enter a void.

His mind projected a segment of his past.

The following vision is one of which that reoccurred frequently ever since the actual encounter as you'll unquestionably realize in part two, however, envisioned differently. Bear in mind the dialogue:

It was dark and very windy. The date was September 3rd, 2005. Jeff had just become an official police officer for Dover. However, he had a sick and twisted obsession. He was intrigued by serial killer Jack Rebus. He didn't idolize nor did he worship him. He was just fascinated with his method of killing and the number of victims he had acquired throughout his short lived spree of morbid belligerence.

Jeff had long since been an author. Albeit he was unsuccessful he pursued it with fervor.

Jeff decided to write a book. His book would be based on the life of Jack Rebus. He even had a working title: The Devil's Soul. Simple but catchy.

Anyway, destined to sell millions of copies, Jeff had to gain as much information as possible. He had to get into the state penitentiary and interview Jack. He used his badge to gain access and control over the prison's regulations.

Jeff wanted to know everything down to the most macabre detail.

"Why did you kill? What made you kill?"

"Power. Control. Envy. Lust." Jack gave a variety of simple answers and grinned sadistically between each word.

"What was your weapon of choice? I mean, the papers said you killed them by strangulation. Did you ever use any weapons other than your bare hands?"

"Cop, do you believe everything you hear? They killed themselves. I was the little voice inside their heads."

"Did you ever feel regret?"

"Regret means you're sorry. It shows weakness. I am not weak nor am I sorry."

"What made you want to kill?"

Jack turned to Jeff with a gleam in his eye grinned sadistically and said, "You."

Physically Jeff still stood in the shower. Mentally Jeff relived this encounter.

Between the illustrations of thought black gaps blossomed separating segments.

Jeff was now at his house—alone. He stood by his typewriter acting strangely. He acted out a possible dramatization using a pillow as a victim. He pretended to be Jack Rebus. The hypothesis here is that Jeff was trying to get inside the mind of Jack. Using the information he had gathered from the interview he became so obsessed as to enact certain presumptions.

To the public and his co-workers, Jeff was well respected and appeared normal. But when he was in the privacy of his own home he acted out. As eccentric as a writer may be Jeff defined the daftness in creativity.

Chapter Two

Jeff and Dale took the Explorer. The whole precinct was headed out to Lake Hummingbird to tear down a marijuana crop. Jeff drove.

On the way to the lake, Dale said, "You don't think any less of me, do ya?"

Jeff seemed dumbfounded. He responded by saying, "What?"

"You know, about what I told you a couple of days ago?"

Still, Jeff was befuddled. "Dale, I have the slightest idea what you mean."

"Okay, drop it. Dang."

Dale was referring to the night at the bar when he explained to Jeff his inability to shoot someone. This didn't seem like Jeff—to forget something so soon. Dale knew this. Therefore, Dale began to question his own sanity. He convinced himself that he must've imagined himself telling Jeff his secret.

When they arrived at the lake everyone exited their vehicle.

Everyone was in uniform except for Jeff and Dale. They wore leisure.

The Cannabis was not hidden at all. It was in plain sight—bushels upon bushels. They got their tools and together made an effort to tear down the plants and destroy the crop. There was a full year's tuition, maybe even a down payment on a nice house valued in the abundance of the crop.

It wasn't their concern.

They enjoyed every bit of tearing it down.

Meanwhile, Linda sat alone beneath the veranda. She read Doyle's: A Study in Scarlet—a Sherlock Holmes mystery. She appeared content as she turned the page.

She was fully unaware of the presence that stood not three feet from her.

He was a young man well groomed and leisurely dressed. In his hand, he held a notebook.

"Ma'am," he broke the silence.

Linda jolted. "Yes, and you are?"

"I'm from the newspaper. I was hoping to get an article written on the marijuana crop being destroyed. Jeff Roberts does live here, correct?"

"Yes, but he's working. He won't be home for a while. I'll be sure to tell him you stopped by."

He said, "Okay," as he handed her his card and continued by saying, "you do that."

She looked at it as he sauntered away.

"Media hounds," Linda said as she wadded up the card and threw it in a nearby wastebasket.

The card displayed the name, Stedman.

Before he exited the veranda completely he turned and asked, "You are his wife, correct?"

She responded with a forbearing nod indicating yes.

He left.

She proceeded to read her book.

While working in the heat Jeff became exhausted. He told Dale and the others that he was going to take a break. He went to the Explorer to cool off. He turned his AC on to the maximum setting. As he sat there he began to get too comfortable. Before too long he was sound asleep.

He dreamed that he was at the prison—standing in the hall. Jack Rebus stood beside him. Jeff held a bloody knife in his hand as Jack held onto a decapitated head by its hair. Correctional Officers walked by casually as if nothing was wrong. Then, suddenly, Jack looked at Jeff and grinned with his sadistic smirk. But, then, Jack was gone. Jeff stood alone with the knife in his right hand and the head in his left hand. He now grinned sadistically the same as Jack.

A knock sounded loudly on the window of the Explorer. Jeff awoke. He looked out the window and saw Dale.

"Finished," said Dale.

"What time is it?" asked Jeff still half asleep.

"A quarter till…."

"You let me sleep for a whole hour?"

"You needed it. You looked warn out," Dale said as he climbed into the passenger seat.

Jeff turned over the ignition and pulled out of the lot.

"Where to?" asked Jeff.

"I gotta get home."

"Yeah, me too. The wife will kill me if I stay out late again. I'm running out of excuses."

"You mean you lie to her?"

"She doesn't approve of my drinking. She mentioned an ultimatum."

Dale quickly changed the subject. "Well, we got rid of one crop…three more to go."

"We'll get 'em."

Apparently, Jeff didn't like talking about his personal affairs no more than Dale wanted to hear about them. Jeff responded to Dale quicker than it took Dale to change the subject. They say: *great minds think alike*. In this case, the adage held true.

Jeff drove down the highway and headed home. The sky ahead of them looked as if it was turning black. It morphed into phases from blue to midnight blue to gray then, a darker shade of gray—marbling.

They managed to get done just before the storm.

Chapter Three

Jeff wore a huge, charcoal trench coat with his badge on the lapel. He was characterized mostly by torrid emotion—especially during heated conversations.

He and Dale sat in his office and discussed a current spree of robberies.

Jeff took his job seriously and throve to be the best at what he did.

For the past couple of days, a bank and three stores had been subject to robbery. The assailants had not yet been identified. Surveillance cameras caught them in the act. However, they wore disguises.

Dale and Jeff were discussing the perpetrators' methods of theft while going over the video. They were talking about how nothing was coming together.

Jeff didn't believe that the four burglaries were connected. He conceived the notion that the bank was an inside job—separate from the stores.

Jeff was usually right. Dale came to expect that.

Dale always came in second. He was aware of this. However, he knew Jeff for the past three years and had grown very close. Also, Jeff was good at what he did. He deserved to get all the admiration.

Everyone wanted Jeff's attention including a meddlesome columnist by the name of Stedman. He had been looking for Jeff ever since they destroyed the marijuana crops. He appeared at Jeff's house one night last week when Jeff wasn't home and spoke to his wife. However, she assured him that she would give Jeff the message. Apparently, it slipped her mind.

Jeff was unaware of Stedman's interest in a story—very unaware.

When Stedman approached Jeff at the station Jeff was totally caught off guard.

Stedman assumed that Jeff was expecting him. That, however, was not the reality.

Jeff looked at him with a vague expression on his face.

"It's Stedman. My name is Stedman. I saw your wife last week. She not mention me?"

"No. What do you want?"

"I just wanted to ask you some questions about the marijuana crop you guys found."

"Crops. They were crops."

"Oops, I apologize."

"Oh, you're one of them. What paper do you work for?"

"I'm local. The Dover Advocate."

Jeff looked up at Dale. "Dale, give us a few minutes."

"Sure thing, Boss," replied Dale as he exited the office. He sometimes referred to Jeff as "Boss" when he felt that Jeff was being too bossy.

"Go on," said Jeff as he nodded at Stedman to proceed.

Stedman reached into his pocket and grabbed his recorder. He pressed the record button and placed it on the edge of a table that was next to them.

Jeff suddenly felt a slight unease—almost as if he was being interrogated. "Let's get this over with. I got things to do." Jeff sounded unhappy about being interviewed; yet, he was willing.

Stedman proceeded to question Jeff about the marijuana crops. Meanwhile, Dale stood on the outside looking in.

Dale envied Jeff.

Later that night, Linda stood near her garden staring at a citronella tiki torch and its coruscant flame. The flame would coruscate even more every time a bug would hover near.

She was mesmerized by the sparks and crackles.

A coruscant flame is a lively flame—bright with colors and resilient in movement.

It seemed the longer she gazed at the flame the more resilient it became.

The sparks and crackles were exuberant—almost like a miniature fireworks' display.

The coruscant flame put Linda into a state of hypnosis.

Someone watched her from the bushes.

The peeper was as mesmerized by her as she was the flame. And as she gazed at the flame there wasn't a thing in this world that would break her concentration.

She envisioned herself dancing around the flame, then, within the flame. Engulfed in the brilliance of its beauty she was the flame.

Suddenly, a hand reached over her shoulder. And the hand caressed her shoulder firmly as she stood undisturbed. She cupped her soft and petite touch over the stranger's large and course hand.

She knew that grasp.

A woman knows her lover's touch.

It was Jeff.

He spoke softly into her ear.

Together, they adjourned to the bedroom.

As they slid beneath the covers the flame went out leaving a smoldering wick. Its glow was a lustrous red.

Chapter Four

Nothing changed for the better. In fact, things only worsened.

Two weeks had elapsed and Jeff's drinking problem was exacerbated. Linda was completely fed up. She was riled to no end by his lies. And he had his excuses too.

—I'm not feeling well. I must have the flu.

—Dale and I were out so late last night working on a case. I'm plumb exhausted.

—My ulcer must be acting up. Maybe, it's my gallbladder.

—This case is stressing me out.

—I just need a break is all.

Jeff had so many excuses. His plan was to cover all basis—his late night outs, his nausea, his sensation of vertigo, and overall drunkenness. He was usually still in a stupor when he fed her the bullshit. She knew better. However, she was afraid to say too much for fear their relationship would end in jeopardy.

She loved him very much—much too much.

Jeff knew that he was causing his beloved emotional infliction. But he just kept digging deeper. Metaphorically he was digging the hole for which he intended to bury his wife in—the hole being her mental frustration—bury, meaning the destruction of one another's affinity.

Jeff didn't seem to care. He saw it coming. And it was traveling at warp speed.

On this particular night, Jeff came home. And he was soused—drunker than Cooter Brown. Needless to say, Linda was at the end of her rope with what-to-do contrivances.

They argued.

"What's your excuse this time? Dammit, Jeff. What is it?"

He smiled drunkenly and staggered against the doorway. He had not yet crossed the threshold. "Good times is all. Good times."

"Dammit, Jeff! I need an answer!" Linda expressed strong emotion.

"So what? What now?"

"I dunno. You tell me."

"Ya want me gone? D'ya want me to get the fuck out of your life?"

"Don't do this, Jeff. Not now. I'm near my breaking point."

"Then, snap! I'm out!"

Linda broke down with an upsurge of potent feelings.

Jeff was on his way, lurching up the stairs, to gather his things. She knew right then it was over.

She didn't have to remind him of the ultimatum.

In a sense, he was already gone.

Linda hoped that he would pass out upstairs and wake up in the morning remembering nothing.

She waited for ten minutes, pacing back and forth restlessly before she decided to go up and check on him.

She met him halfway.

He held a huge duffel bag overflowing with clothing.

"Can we talk?" asked Linda through her weeping exhales and quivering lips.

"There's nothing to talk about," Jeff replied with slurred speech and a hiccup between *nothing* and *to*.

"We need to talk things through. Where do you plan on going?" By now, Linda was distraught and questioned Jeff's every move.

"I have money. There are plenty of motels."

"Jeff, I can't let you go."

Jeff seemed heartless. "It's not my concern."

As he walked toward the door he grabbed his badge from a small table.

Linda didn't stand in his way.

Jeff made it to his car and, before long, was pulling out of the driveway.

She knew that she wouldn't sleep that night. She knew that she was too riled with emotion. Also, she knew she needed someone to talk to—a confidant. The only person that came to mind was a college acquaintance she had met while studying to be a nurse. His name was Ted. She had managed to stay in touch with him through Facebook.

She got online and chatted with him. Eventually, he invited himself to her house. Within an hour he arrived.

Linda answered the door and was pleased to see Ted standing before her. She was still disconcerted.

Together, side by side, they sat on the couch.

"What's wrong, Linda? What did he do?"

"He didn't do anything. It's me. All me." Linda blamed herself in order to sustain more pity.

Ted consoled her. However, he acted as if he was less concerned in regards to her emotional spill—typical male. He supported her, true. By doing so he took advantage of her vulnerability.

She rested her head upon his shoulder as he lightly stroked her hair.

They still talked.

He made a failed attempt at persuading her into believing that Jeff was a jerk. She still blamed herself. Nothing could convince her otherwise.

She didn't call on Ted to be convinced that Jeff was one-hundred percent in the wrong and to be reminded of his insensitivity. She just needed a friend. If she had any female acquaintances she would have called on one of them.

Ted had other intentions.

Linda was not at all promiscuous but Ted, quickly, produced wanton behavior. Knowing that she was overly relaxed he gently placed her head upon his lap. Still, he stroked her hair. He would gingerly pull her hair upward, feeling the long strands that slid through his fingers. As he did this he also snuffed her hair, complimenting her shampoo and conditioner.

Linda drifted into a torpid state of rest.

A set of headlights appeared in the driveway. It was Jeff returning home. Apparently, he had forgotten something and came home just long enough to grab it.

He was still drunk.

He noticed the strange car as he walked past it. He made the comment, "Is that my car?" which didn't make much sense, but considering his state of mind the dynamics of perception are not relevant to interpretation. However, Jeff would soon discover the answer.

16

On each side of the front door were long panels of slender windows. The curtains were thin and, with enough light, one could see right through them with great clarity.

Jeff saw Ted sitting on the couch. Also, he noticed Linda's foot with her tattered gown wrapping around it just above the ankle. But where was the rest of Linda? From Jeff's angle, it left little to the imagination. He was forced to draw his own conclusion. Jeff's sense of emotion was heightened from the alcohol he had consumed earlier. His assumption was Linda committed an adulterous act.

He left.

He stormed to his car with tempestuous movements. He pulled out, nearly backing into a tree, and drove recklessly. His intent was never to return. Although, he had yet to sober.

Maybe a good night's rest and temperance would change his attitude.

Maybe he would remember none of this by morning.

Chapter Five

Jeff awoke in a bed all alone.

Linda was nowhere around.

Slightly confused he knew what had happened. However, he remembered seeing Linda in coitus with her beau. So, he thought. You and I both know the truth of the matter. Jeff only *knew* what he *thought* he saw.

Jeff acknowledged that he had screwed up. Linda, however, destroyed the only chance of his coming back home. A stupid decision on her part was to invite over a male acquaintance to soothe her woe.

What's a man supposed to think?

He was overwrought with grief.

The room was small and filled with cockroaches. For the price he paid, there was no sense in complaining.

He lay in his bed and flicked through the channels. The television set was small and outdated. The only thing on was infomercials and reruns of old shows. After three consecutive rounds of flicking through every channel the low-budget network had to offer he decided to settle with an episode of Dr.

Jekyll and Mr. Hyde he swore he had never seen. Quickly he became content with the plot.

His cell phone rang. The ringtone was Bad Boys by Inner Circle. He knew right away that it was Dale.

"Yeah."

"Got some great news, man, and you're gonna love it."

"I could use some 'bout now." By the tone of Jeff's voice, Dale knew something was wrong.

"The bank robber and the store bandits were both caught this morning. Well, the bank robber turned himself in, but the store bandits were apprehended while robbing another store."

"Good deal. What's their bail?"

"Don't know yet. We're still trying to figure everything out down here. Where are you?"

"Penny's One Night Stay."

"What are you doing there? You didn't leave Linda for a hooker did you?" Dale laughed out a short burst.

"Partly."

Dale instantly became more serious. "What d'ya mean?"

"I came home drunk last night and me and Linda had it out. I left. Look, there's much more to the story. I'd feel better talking to you in person. In private."

"Okay, cool. I'll be right there. What's your room number?"

"26 B."

Dale chuckled, "I know 26 B."

"I'm sure you do."

"All right, man. Gimme an hour. I'll be there."

"And I'll be here waiting."

Soon after their conversation ended his phone rang again. This time the ringtone was When I Look into Your Eyes by Firehouse, which was Linda's ringtone. Jeff chuckled morosely. With everything that was going on, he couldn't hold up to those feelings. He now saw Linda in a whole new light.

He ignored the phone call. It wasn't but a couple of minutes later When I Look into Your Eyes rang out again. Jeff had just become refocused on the show. This time he answered.

A softly spoken voice said, "Can we talk? Do you have time for me?"

Jeff didn't know what to say. Overall, their conversation merged into an argument about Linda and her male visitor the night before. Linda was awestricken by Jeff's accusations. She admitted to having Ted over but strongly denied anything sexual.

Jeff had a lot to think about. He had always known Linda to be an honest Southern Belle. What was he thinking? Perhaps he was blinded by misperception and chose to create a false attribute to place the guilt on his wife. Maybe it was the alcohol. Either way, Linda delivered a concise message. She said very little; however, her point was candid.

Also, she explained to Jeff that her father was ill. The doctor had diagnosed him with leukemia and he was given less than a week to live. She told Jeff that she would feel negligible if she didn't see him, at least once, before he died. She added that she may even decide to stay in Rappaport so she could show her support and be there to assist with funeral arrangements. That's where her father lived—Rappaport—which was a sixty-mile drive east of Dover. She continued to explicate that she didn't expect Jeff to come with her with all the occurring burglaries and such. She assured Jeff that they could work things out upon her return.

Jeff sympathized with Linda, but at the same time, he was happy to know that he was welcomed to come back home. Already he had missed his bed.

Immediately after their conversation Jeff called Dale and told him not to bother coming over. He explained that he and Linda had agreed to work things out and that he was packing his things to head back home. Dale was happy for Jeff but saddened to hear the dreadful news about Linda's father. He told Jeff, "It's a good thing you guys are gonna fight this out. She needs you right now more than ever."

Jeff concurred by saying, "Yeah, God does work in mysterious ways."

Chapter Six

Curtis Blackwell lived on the edge of Mulberry Lane. His house was old and skeevy in appearance. It was a two-story Victorian-style house with an iron fence that wrapped around every inch of the yard. At that, the fence itself looked like it belonged in a cemetery.

Every kid in Dover had been warned, at least once, to stay away from Curtis Blackwell's place. Did they listen?—of course not. And Curtis knew the kids feared him as much as the rest of the community loathed him. Yet, he was frequently bothered by the children. Albeit the children feared him they were curious as to see his face.

Curtis Blackwell was a hermit—a recluse—a troglodyte. However, some believed him to be an anchorite. In order to be an anchorite one must bear religious beliefs. That's what Granny Picket, a little old lady across the yard from Curtis, rumored. For months she had the town convinced that he used to be a monk driven from his cloister. She added: *He sexually abused small children.*

Others even accused him of being a vampire. The children were most gullible to deem that as true. Be it as it may, Curtis was nothing more than a lonely old man. He was antisocial and chose to live a life of seclusion. He had his reasons. Later, you'll see why.

In Curtis Blackwell's back yard sat an old, rusty pickup truck. It was a classic, however, in poor condition. The city alderman was cracking down on unlicensed vehicles and, on the whole, filthy yards. Curtis had a very clean yard—vibrant green grass, trimmed hedges, and even a few variations of flowers here and there. But it was his old and rusty truck that caused him all the grief.

The alderman made several attempts at paying him many visits but Curtis would never respond to his door chime or any other effort to get his attention. Therefore, the alderman turned him over to the police.

This, of course, would give Granny Picket great pleasure to see and much to talk about.

The sky hung filthy gray curtains. It looked as if it urged to storm badly, but the hot and cold battled and produced a vapor that teased the sky.

Dale got out of his patrol car and vigilantly walked through the gate of Curtis Blackwell's ominous domain. Once Dale approached the front door he gave the primitive façade the onceover.

After five loud knocks, Curtis answered the door. His reply was, "Oh, Officer Dale Wilson. Do come in." Dale was waiting to hear: *I've been expecting you.* The man's voice was somewhat sinister. And Dale had seen way too many horror movies.

Dale stood stiffly and measured Curtis with accipitrine eyes. Curtis was very tall and had a stalwart physique. Also, he was completely bald. His face narrowed outward like a vulture. His eyes squinted inward like a wildcat.

Not too many people had actually ever seen Curtis. Some claimed to have seen him but, to Dale, he looked nothing like the descriptions he had heard.

Dale stared at him hard to create a mental profile of the man most people feared in Dover.

The one question flourished in Dale's mind: *Why did he invite me in when he ignores everyone else?*

Then, Curtis said, "I've been expecting you." It was about that time Dale was ready, willing, and able to leave. He figured: *I might as well get while the getting's good.* However, Dale had a job to do. And Dale backed down from nothing—most of the time.

"Mr. Blackwell, I've had many complaints about the truck you have back there. Getting it licensed is clearly not an option seeing its condition and all. Therefore, you can either dispose of it yourself or the city will tow it at your expense."

Curtis didn't look too happy. "How long do I have?"

"I can give you till the end of the month."

"That won't be a problem. I have a son that will be coming down from Belleworth. Do you know where that is, Dale?"

"I'm not for sure."

"It's on the other side of Kentucky heading west. His boy, my grandson, was just killed in Iraq…fighting the war. Yeah, with my son away and my only grandson with the angels, I guess the only thing I have left are my flowers. That's all I seem to care about anymore is my flowers…and my precious roses. That grandkid of mine wanted to follow in my footsteps. I dodged many-a-bullet. I guess the war can spare a life or claim a life. I fought at Vietnam, ya know. How I made it? That's a question I've never been able to answer. I guess I had a guardian angel looking out for me. Do you believe in angels, Dale?"

Dale was confused. What did any of this have to do with Curtis removing his truck from his yard? Curtis entered his own dimension of thought. Dale decided to just go along. He found Curtis to be an interesting character. "Umm, I guess."

Curtis started to explain to Dale the origin of angels. Dale's attention began to drift away. His eyes wandered. Curtis had so many neat things lying around—artifacts, antiques, and war memorabilia. However, one thing really grabbed Dale's attention. On one of the walls, Curtis displayed, what appeared to be, shrunken heads. They were attached to jute and were very noticeable. Intrigued Dale stared at the well-preserved heads, which stared back at him.

Curtis sensed Dale's interest. "Got 'em in Korea. They're supposed to bring good health and longevity. I feel as though I'm in good physical shape for my age. I have the heart of a lion."

Dale regained attention. "They're different." He paused a second, looked at Curtis and said, "Welp, I gotta go."

Curtis fighting in Vietnam and losing his grandson to a war was the reason for his state of mild insanity and seclusion. Not too many were aware of his hardship. They chose to pass on hearsay with loose ends and add to the bruited slander. But the fact that he displayed shrunken heads upon his wall frightened the hell out of Dale. He didn't know whether to tell someone or bottle the information. The poor man needed a break. That was all he needed was for folks to gossip that he had decapitated heads hanging in his house.

Dale chose to only tell Jeff. Jeff was exceptional at keeping secrets. At that, Jeff had a few skeletons in his closet, as well.

Chapter Seven

Jeff was enjoying his time alone. He was confident that everything was okay between him and Linda.

She was still in Rappaport and planning her dad's funeral.

Jeff would go on his early morning jogs and, then, go to work. He would stay up late reading. He had no restrictions. However, he did miss his wife. Linda made him feel whole. She encouraged him to do so much. They belonged together.

On this particular morning, Jeff was preparing for a jog when Dale showed up.

"Getting ready to go for a jog?" Dale asked.

"Yes, and I feel great. I slept so good last night," replied Jeff.

"Well, I got something to tell ya."

"About?"

"It's about Curtis Blackwell."

That really grabbed Jeff's attention. "You mean the freak of Dover?"

"If you wanna call him that. Look, I went to his house yesterday."

"You were in his house!?!"

"Yes. And he had a lot to say." Jeff looked at Dale intrigued as if he anticipated hearing something interesting. Dale continued, "He told me something. He said to me, 'I guess the war can spare a life or claim a life.' He was in the war, Jeff. The Vietnam-fucking-war."

"That says a lot. Most folks that come out of Nam are better off dead. I would not want to live the rest of my life as one big blur." Jeff referred to reoccurring flashbacks that most war veterans suffer from due to their traumatic and near death experiences.

Dale nodded his head in agreement. In his mind, he debated on whether or not he should tell Jeff about the shrunken heads. He made a quick decision not to.

It wasn't long before Dale left. He told Jeff he needed to go home and freshen up. Soon after Dale pulled out of the driveway Jeff ran out the door slowing down to a snail's pace once he hit the pavement.

Jeff reached the turnoff to Mulberry Lane. He usually jogged past it. The only two houses on that road were Granny Picket's and Curtis Blackwell's.

Jeff would rather not have anything to do with either one of them. However, his conscience spoke to him.

He turned and headed down Mulberry Lane.

He stopped in front of Curtis Blackwell's ominous house. He stared at it with much curiosity. He wondered if the inside was as eerie as the outside. Dale knew. That's when it dawned on him. Rather than snooping he would confront Dale later at work and ask him. Dale would tell him everything he needed to know. So, he thought.

Jeff entered his office and collapsed into his chair. He was worn out. He gently laid his forehead on his desk and pulled his cell phone from within his pant pocket. He flipped it open and fiddled with the keypad as he looked down at it with his forehead resting upon his desk. It appeared as if he was preparing to call his wife when Dale entered.

"You wanted to see me, Boss?" said Dale.

Jeff quickly closed his phone and slid it back into his pocket. "Yeah, actually I do. Sit down." Jeff pointed at a chair as he stood up. He paced around the room. "You were inside Curtis Blackwell's place, correct?"

Dale gulped. "Yeah." He just knew that Jeff was going to pull every strand of information out of him—including the shrunken heads.

"Explain to me some of the—"

Dale interrupted him and spilled the beans. "Okay, he has this weird collection of shrunken heads. He claimed to have gotten them from Korea or somewhere. He said, 'They're supposed to bring good health and longevity.' It's a likable story."

It was Jeff's turn to interrupt. He belted out a loud laugh. "Dale, I have no clue or interest in what you're talking about. This isn't Plainfield and he's far from Ed Gein. Shoot, the man is just misunderstood. You can buy shrunken heads off the internet. They look so doggone real. I doubt they're real." Then, he began to question his own state of mind. "They're not real, are they?"

"Couldn't tell ya. I stared at 'em for a while. I didn't get too close. I mean, they looked real. I dunno, Jeff. Hell, what're shrunken heads supposed ta look like, anyway?"

"Heads that are little, shrunken, little shriveled up heads…" Jeff stumbled over his own words as he tried to give a detailed description.

Dale snickered.

Jeff got a serious look on his face. "We need to get a closer look at those heads."

"I'm not going in there. Are you freaking crazy? I experienced that once. If you want 'em that bad go alone."

"C'mon, bud. It'll be like a Sherlock Holmes mystery: Case of the Shrunken Heads. Let's do it."

As mentioned before Dale was easily manipulated—especially by Jeff. Therefore, Dale nodded his head and said, "Let's do this!"

Chapter Eight

It was 12:30 in the afternoon. Jeff and Dale needed a plan. All they needed was one shrunken head. However, they needed to get Curtis out of his house for at least fifteen minutes. That would be impossible.

Curtis never left his house.

Suddenly, Dale had an idea. He said, "Let's pull some of his flowers in the back yard there and run them over to Granny Picket's front porch. We'll set them in plain sight. We'll knock on his back door and run behind that big oak tree over there." Dale pointed in the direction of the tree. "If all goes well he'll see that they're scattered on her porch and go over to her house and confront her about destroying his precious flowers."

"Dammit, Dale! That was the dumbest idea I have ever heard," Jeff said loudly at first as he quickly lowered his voice.

The two acted like children trying to pull off a clever Halloween prank.

Then, Dale explained to Jeff: "Jeff, Curtis told me, 'That's all I seem to care about anymore is my flowers.' Trust me. This will work."

Jeff took his word for it. Besides, what did they have to lose? Oh yeah, their lives. But Dale was confident in his plan and Jeff had balls of steel. They could very well pull this off.

Together they quietly entered Curtis Blackwell's fence and crept against the side of his house. Before too long they were in the back yard at the edge of his house staring at a bushel of roses.

Dale didn't waste any time.

Jeff didn't participate much. He just stood there staring at Dale as if to say: *You have lost your mind.*

Dale grabbed two big handfuls, crushed them in his hands, and threw them on the ground. Then, he grabbed two more big handfuls. "Let's go," Dale said as Jeff nonchalantly followed.

If Linda only knew the hijinks they were getting into while she was away.

With feet like a ninja, they hightailed it over to Granny Picket's house. And as the saying goes: so far, so good.

Dale quickly scattered the roses upon Granny Picket's front porch. It looked awful like a wild animal had dug them up and strewn them.

Now they had one less feat to accomplish. They had to go back over to Curtis Blackwell's, knock, and hide behind the tree.

Dale and Jeff fussed back and forth over a suggestion Dale had made to Jeff. Dale said, "You knock on the door. I destroyed the roses." And that's what started the argument.

After a good minute long dispute Jeff caved. He said, "Okay, let's get this over with. I'm missing Reno 911."

Dale uttered a short snicker, "You watch that show?"

"Did I say Reno 911? I meant CSI."

"Ha, CSI isn't even on tonight."

It was pointless arguing with Dale.

This very moment exemplified their nature toward one another.

Then, side by side, the two walked back over to the ominous house like they were on a mission and in total control.

Dale went ahead and hid behind the tree. He wasn't being a coward. He just wanted Jeff to have a clean cut-and-run without tripping over his partner in crime—smart thinking on Dale's behalf.

Jeff knocked very loudly. So loud Jeff barely made it behind the tree before Curtis stepped out on his back porch.

Curtis saw red. He clinched his fists and said, "Those damn dogs!" Then, he went around every window to avoid coming out at first and looked to see if he saw any animals making off with his precious roses. He had no luck. However, when he did look out his front door he saw his roses. They were scattered all over Granny Picket's front porch.

Immediately Curtis slammed open his front door and walked over to Granny Picket's house with tempestuous movements.

Dale and Jeff seized the opportunity.

They wasted no time at all.

Already they were in the house. Jeff stood by the door and watched as Dale went straight to the shrunken heads. Dale knew exactly where they were.

Dale latched onto one and pulled it off the wall. However, with the head in his hand, he noticed small letters carved in the back toward the bottom. They spelled out: MADE IN KOREA.

Dale picked up another, and, then, another. It was unbelievable. They all said the same thing. They even felt like plastic.

All that trouble for nothing.

Jeff and Dale made a narrow escape just before Curtis returned home.

What an experience.

Chapter Nine

As mentioned earlier Dale confessed to Jeff that he couldn't shoot a man. Of course, Dale had to remind him. So one morning the two of them took the day off. Their plans were to meet out at Jeff's father's old farmhouse. His dad had long since been deceased. During Jeff's free time, he turned the old barn into an indoor shooting range.

Dale had held a gun on many occasions and may have shot inanimate objects once or twice. He was very well oriented with the use of the weapon. However, Jeff figured if he could get Dale to fire it ten to fifteen times every other day that his fear of using his gun would eventually wane. And at first, Dale was all for it. But to stand six feet from the target and hold the heavy Glock in his hand put him on edge.

Day 1: Dale fired the first shot. He even fired a second shot. He brought to Jeff's attention that he didn't see this being a beneficial method of overcoming his fear. Jeff told him to hang in there and take it slow. He explained to Dale how he had a few extra ideas but he chose to do it all in phases. Dale didn't like it when Jeff spoke of a few extra ideas let alone "phases."

But it was fun.

Linda was still in Rappaport. Dale had no place to be. The crime rate was at an all-time low. Therefore, Dale and Jeff enjoyed every bit of the time they got to bond.

And for Dale to have a fear of shooting someone with his gun he proved to be an excellent marksman. Jeff was awestricken. Dale told Jeff that he could shoot the gun all day. But in a situation where he had to shoot or be shot, he would fail.

At one point Dale aimed for the mid-section of the target. His shot went clean through to the other side of the barn. However, they heard a loud and shrieking cat's meow. It was comical how they both turned at the exact time and looked at each other like: *What just happened?* They both ran around the building and that cat managed to jump onto the side of the barn with its huge extended claws embedded in the wood. They laughed hysterically at how that poor calico held on for dear life.

They had so much fun.

They went from shooting paper targets inside the range to aluminum beer and cola cans Jeff found lying around. Jeff would even fill them full of grit and throw them way up in the sky like clay disks. Still, Dale shot every single one—impressive.

However, all good things must come to an end. Once they ran out of bullets the fun was over.

Day 2: they went back out to the farmhouse. This time Jeff had conjured up a more difficult task. He picked up a dozen melons and had planned on standing off to the side while chucking them toward Dale so that he could shoot them.

Dale didn't miss a single melon.

He shot one and it busted into a puree showering Jeff with melon sauce and tiny seed fragments.

Now they were having way too much fun.

Suddenly, Jeff came up with an even greater task. He would tie a melon to a rope, climb into the hayloft, and swing them at Dale with a great amount of force. He wouldn't give the slightest warning. This would test Dale's reaction time.

Out of five melons, Dale managed to only shoot one. Jeff joked and said he would give him an A for effort. Dale joked back and said he felt more like he deserved an A-plus. Jeff admired Dale's confidence but told him not to get ahead of himself. He had many more great ideas in store.

Day 3: the day before Jeff came out to the farmhouse on his motorcycle without Dale and made some scarecrows with sticks running through the backs of them. Dale didn't know what he had coming to him. But Jeff was clever. He made the sticks angle out so that he would be out of the line of fire.

Jeff was going through a lot of trouble over this. However, he didn't consider it any trouble at all. Once again they felt like two kids having fun— just like when they were breaking into Curtis Blackwell's place.

Dale didn't have any problem at all shooting those scarecrows.

Jeff was at wit's end. How far would he take this? How far would he go to help Dale overcome his fear of shooting someone in the line of defense? Then, a big smile stretched across Jeff's face. Dale didn't like that one bit.

Day 4: they exited the Explorer. Jeff held a bag in his hand. Dale didn't know what to expect.

Jeff instructed Dale to go ahead and get the gun loaded and ready. He told Dale that he was going to go and get something set up.

Dale was befuddled.

Soon out stepped Jeff. Dale looked downward at the gun and was unaware of Jeff's presence. But when he looked up he was in disarray. There stood Jeff in a bullet proof vest. By now Dale was ready to go on home and call it a day.

Jeff tried to convince Dale that this is what they did while he was in training. He said, "It stings a bit but nothing major. No one has ever died doing this that I know of." Still, that was not enough to convince Dale.

Dale strongly replied, "I'm not shooting my friend, you idiot!"

"Trust me, Dale. I wouldn't allow you to do it if I knew it meant getting hurt." Jeff was wasting his breath. Dale would not cave. "Oh well, let's head on back into town…maybe some other day when you got the nerve." That did it.

Dale said, "Get over there."

Jeff made sure he was at least ten feet away from the blast. He urged Dale to aim vigilantly.

Dale had him locked in his sights.

His finger was on the trigger.

The gun was cocked and loaded.

All Dale had to do was pull the hammer down.

Sweat formed on his forehead and glistened as he entered a slight state of tremors.

He couldn't do it. "I haven't got the nerve," he said as he unlocked his arm and set the gun down on a nearby sawhorse.

"Don't worry. We'll figure it out," assured Jeff.

Dale felt like a child being comforted by his older brother.

They climbed into the Explorer and pulled out. Once they were on the dirt road they disappeared through the scattered dust.

Chapter Ten

Jeff awoke to the soothing sound of Linda's ringtone. Immediately he answered. He looked to his right as he still lay in bed at his digital clock. It was 5:30 AM.

With a gravelly croak, Jeff spoke, "Hey, babe."

"Jeff, can you hear me?" Linda spoke loudly with her voice embedded within static.

"A little but you're cutting out some." Jeff sat up on the edge of the bed.

"Okay. I'll call back later." That's what Linda said. What Jeff heard was: "...kay...ack...ater," with the ellipsis points representing static-interference. However, he inferred her message clearly.

Jeff decided to get up and stir around a bit. It was very early and Jeff was extremely groggy. He and Dale had been having too much fun. Between just hanging out and helping Dale with his shooting he needed a day to himself. And he planned just that.

Jeff went out his back door and entered the shed where he kept his motorcycle. It was a 1980 Harley Davidson XLS Roadster. He sat on it and got ready to start it. Suddenly, Dale walked through the door.

Dale didn't want anything in particular. He just stopped by for a visit. At that, he left shortly after he arrived—a simple "Hi" and "Bye."

It wasn't too much longer before Linda called back. Jeff responded quickly by answering the cell phone. The reception was so much better. Jeff made out everything she said with the best of clarity almost as if she was standing in the room with him.

"I may be a little longer at getting home," said Linda.

"And why's that?" questioned Jeff.

"Mom is a nervous wreck and Laura, Sara, and Betty and I agreed to pitch in and help her out." The names mentioned are Linda's sisters. They cared less for Linda. They only showed up when they figured money was involved.

They proceeded to talk. Jeff filled Linda in on his misadventures with Dale as Linda did the same with the funeral and such. Eventually, the conversation ended with Linda telling Jeff not to worry. She added that Rappaport is such a small town and nothing ever happens criminal-wise.

Soon after Jeff took a shower. It was still early but he decided to go ahead and stay up the rest of the day. He had done made a mental note of his agenda: go for a jog, fix the lawnmower, and mow the lawn.

Later that day, Jeff was in his shed with the carburetor to his lawnmower disassembled. He received a disturbing phone call. It was from Dale's sister Amanda. She hysterically informed Jeff that Dale had been shot in the shoulder during a foot chase. The assailant committed armed robbery and

Dale was on the scene. Dale had the perfect opportunity to shoot the robber. However, he choked and was shot instead.

According to Amanda Dale had lost a lot of blood.

Jeff thought to himself: *He was just here a little while ago.*

Jeff's hands were caked in grease. He was in disarray and felt as if he hadn't enough time to clean up.

He scooped a glob of Gojo out of the can and scrubbed his hands like the dickens beneath a heavy stream of hot water. However, it wasn't working fast enough. Therefore, Jeff hopped into the Explorer and headed to the hospital with his black greasy hands.

Dale was laid up in his hospital bed with his right shoulder heavily bandaged, an I.V. sticking out of his arm, and a morphine drip.

The expression on Dale's face said more than words to describe his discomfort. And to make matters worse Dale had convinced himself that he had no right to be a cop.

The robber had gotten away.

All Dale had to do was pull the trigger.

Dale seriously doubted his own abilities at being a police officer.

Maybe Jeff could cheer him up.

Jeff carefully sat down next to Dale and spoke quietly. He said, "Hey, bud. Man, I sure hate seeing you like this."

Regardless of the look on his face, Dale was feeling no pain once the relief kicked in. He was high on morphine and found it hard to take anything seriously. Needless to say, Jeff took advantage of his friend's narcotized state of mind and used it for his own amusement.

Jeff tried to explain to Dale the conversation he had with Linda earlier. That didn't happen as he intended it to. Then, Jeff tried to get information out of Dale about the robber. Once more Dale wasn't up to a serious conversation. At that, neither one could keep a straight face.

Eventually, the nurse came in and politely told Jeff that he needed to leave. Jeff respected her authority and did as he was told. However, before he left he told Dale not to get too comfortable. Dale slowly raised his head at Jeff and cracked a crooked smile.

Chapter Eleven

Curtis Blackwell sat in front of his front room window looking out. The view was Granny Picket's house. One could only imagine his state of thought. *What on earth possessed her to ruin my precious flowers?* Still, he was affected by the ordeal.

He furrowed his brow as he traced his lips with his fingertips. He was, indeed, an ominous fellow.

Something was eating at him.

He wouldn't rest easy.

Perhaps he was plotting something.

Curtis watched the old woman as she came out dressed in her Mother Hubbard to feed her cat. She acted as if nothing had ever happened. To her, nothing did happen. It was Jeff and Dale's roguish attempt to get a closer look at Curtis's shrunken head collection that caused this whole ordeal. Even when Granny Picket was confronted by the eerie gargantuan and found the mess of roses at her feet she was near the point of a massive stroke.

She had no clue why he was so upset and talking ugly to her.

She had no clue why his destroyed roses were in her yard.

None of this made any sense to her.

And now she acted as if nothing had ever happened. Maybe she was the crazy one. However, you could tell it still bothered Curtis. He sat and watched her every move. At one point she looked up as if she felt his eyes searing deeply into her soul. He quickly closed his curtain when she did.

His overall intentions were not clear. Curtis wasn't a violent man. But at the same time, he was growing tired of people picking on him—making him the subject matter of all their jokes. Overtime that itself could drive a man crazy.

Jeff left the hospital and had just pulled into his driveway. He noticed a car he had never seen before across the street. He watched it out of the corner of his eye as he grabbed a sack of groceries from the passenger seat. A man exited the car. Immediately Jeff identified him. It was the columnist—Stedman.

Jeff thought aloud but under his chin, "What does he want?"

Stedman approached him and said, "I'm doing a story on the robbery that occurred yesterday. Would you happen to—?"

"You're barking up the wrong tree. The man you need to be speaking to is in the hospital, but now's not a good time."

"Why's that?"

"He was shot. He lost a lot of blood. And if I catch wind that you went there aggravating him I'll be forced to kick your scrawny ass."

Stedman stepped back a couple of feet.

Jeff nonchalantly gave him a smartass grin.

"When would be a good—?"

"Look. If you don't mind. I have a lot of things that need tendin' to. You're not one of them."

Stedman got the point. He walked back to his little car and headed down the road.

Jeff made a quick decision. He didn't care a whole lot for Stedman.

Suddenly, Jeff received a text message on his cell phone. He flipped it open and looked at it. It read: *Dale not doin good. can you come over soon? ~Manda~*. That was Amanda's signature.

Jeff ran his sack of groceries inside the house, put away his perishables, and climbed back into the Explorer.

He almost ran into another car backing out of his driveway before he sped off down the road.

On his way down the road, he replied to the text: *Coming now.*

Jeff was in so much of a hurry he nearly lost control of the wheel—twice. However, he did hone exceptional driving skills.

Back when he was working the beat he encountered many high-speed chases. But this time something went wrong. Needless to say, Jeff didn't make it to the hospital to see Dale.

Jeff blacked out. Maybe his high anxiety level was the cause. Perhaps it was the fear of something going horribly wrong with Dale, and Jeff thought he wouldn't make it on time. Whatever the case things weren't looking well.

Jeff awoke in a hospital bed. He was in pain and very disoriented. At first, it appeared as if he was all alone, which added to his confusion. Then, he heard a familiar voice. It said, "I'm home, baby. I came as soon as I heard about your accident." It was Linda. She stood off to the side barely in sight. Jeff reached out to grab her hand but screamed in pain.

"Come here, Linda. Get over here so that I can see ya," said Jeff.

"Sure, sweetie," replied Linda.

She moved over so that Jeff could see her. She looked lovely.

He was completely taken away by her. And he was happy to see her. However, he wished his seeing her was under different circumstances.

He missed her so much.

However, something didn't quite seem right. Where Linda stood now embodied someone else. It was Granny Picket. Jeff questioned his sanity.

To make things even stranger outside the window stood Curtis Blackwell. He pecked at the window as if he was trying to get someone's attention. None of this was making any sense to Jeff.

Where did Linda go?

Jeff looked around for her. He screamed out her name. She was nowhere around. Then, Jeff saw something he never thought he'd see in a million years. Behind Granny Picket there rose an entity. It was the silhouette of a human form. The shape slowly emerged into focus. It was Jack Rebus.

The sound of a loud shrill fading into a squeaky wheel on a meal cart being pushed down the hall awoke Jeff. He was still in the hospital visiting Dale. Apparently, Jeff had never left the way he had envisioned himself doing so.

It all made sense.

The encounter with Stedman, the blackout, and Linda morphing into Granny Picket and falling victim to Jack Rebus was all a horrible nightmare. But why would Jeff dream up such madness?

Chapter Twelve

Jeff was on his way to Mulberry Lane.

The Dover Police Department received an anonymous tip. Granny Picket had not been seen in two days. Consequently, the caller contacted the police department over their concern. Also, it was mentioned that there was a foul odor coming from her house.

Dale was still recovering at the hospital. Therefore, it was up to Jeff to respond to the call.

Jeff walked around the house. He detected the rancid stench. It was definitely the smell of a dead animal. And the longer Jeff investigated the scene, he found a dead cat—Granny Picket's cat Whiskers.

Granny Picket was frequently heard by surrounding residents, two or three streets over, calling for her cat. Plus, on the day that Jeff and Dale were sneaking into Curtis's house, Jeff noticed that same cat out the corner of his eye sitting comfortably on her front porch.

Jeff inspected the cat closely. Rigor mortis had done set in. However, the cat bared no markings indicating an attack. Jeff kicked at it flipping it over and thought hard to determine a cause of death. Either it died naturally or it was poisoned.

Jack put his investigative skills to use. It was apparent that the cat had been lying in that condition for at least a day. If Granny Picket had known she'd put it in a bag and give it a proper burial. She wouldn't have left it there to stink.

Something didn't seem right.

Jeff made several attempts to knock on the door. Nobody responded to the loud knocks. Then, Jeff felt as if he was being watched. He carefully looked around and noticed a curtain moving over at Curtis Blackwell's house. As bad as Jeff hated to he walked over to visit Curtis. Maybe he knew something.

Jeff knocked loudly upon Curtis's front door.

Jeff would stop in between knocks and admire the primitive façade just as Dale did earlier.

Jeff was not convinced that Curtis was away. He knew Curtis was in there. Curtis, however, was good at ignoring people, especially those who represented authority. Therefore, Jeff took a walk around his house. He looked through every window he could reach and saw nothing. It didn't even appear as if there was any lighting. Then, Jeff made it to the rear edge of the house. He stared at the unsightly rose bush. He released a short and quiet giggle. In a sense, he felt remorse. On the other hand, he and Dale had fun destroying that bush.

He decided to knock on the back door. He knocked for a steady two minutes. His knuckles began to redden and get sore.

Jeff came to the conclusion that he was beating a dead horse. Yet he continued to pounce hoping that Curtis would become annoyed.

Eventually, Jeff got tired of knocking. He decided to go back over to Granny Picket's house.

In order to enter the house he would need a warrant. And if Jeff was certain that he could find something vital he would determine the situation "a probable cause" and enter anyway. Jeff was known for taking chances.

Jeff got lucky. He noticed the back door was slightly cracked. However, he did something stupid. He touched the knob with his bare hand.

He entered the house.

He walked around for less than a minute before he found the old woman. She lay comfortably on her back on her couch. She looked well rested. Jeff knew better. She appeared as stiff as a board. He walked over to investigate further when he noticed a thin trail of bruises that traveled the complete circumference of her neck.

Jeff took a couple of steps back.

He looked around for a murder weapon—preferably a rope. He found nothing. In the meantime, he was putting his prints all over everything. Jeff knew better than this.

Jeff wanted to believe that Granny Picket died of natural causes. Worst yet Jeff compared the current events to his nightmare—the one he had while he was at the hospital visiting Dale. Perhaps it was a premonition.

But beyond the nightmare, Jeff had a deeper concern. The crime scene resembled, in many ways, one that he remembered seeing in a photograph six years ago. The victim's name was Macie Brown.

Chapter Thirteen

It was 6:30 PM. Jeff was sorting through a box of old odds and ends. He had just finished talking to Linda over the telephone.

She was on her way home.

Dale was doing better at the hospital—awaiting to be discharged. But Jeff was feeling weary. He missed Linda, albeit, was happy to hear she was coming home.

The box contained memories—good and bad. He sorted through photos and had two juxtaposed on an end table. They were of him of different ages.

Jeff was in the mood to reminisce. He had a bottle of Jack Daniels beside him, however, resisted his thirsty urge.

Jeff dug and dug through the box as if he was looking for something in particular. Maybe he was looking for wedding photos. Perhaps he was looking for a video. It was not yet certain.

Suddenly, he stopped.

He looked into the box like he was staring at a freak show oddity. Then, he reached into the box. He pulled out a scrapbook that was labeled: *Exhibit A*. He reacted in a felicitous manner toward his discovery.

He thumbed through the scrapbook intrigued by every page.

Suddenly, he stopped.

He stared at a photograph with an intent look. It was a little boy dressed in a yellow polo shirt (the kind with the crocodile stitched in over the pocket) and a pair of worn out corduroy pants.

After staring at the photo for a while he closed the scrapbook and set it on the couch beside him.

He began to dig in the box again.

He travailed at this—a day long effort.

Then, he found something that really sparked his attention with heartfelt warmth. He found a receipt from Marty's GameRoom. The date on the receipt was 9/4/2005. That was the night he and Linda met. That single piece of grease-stained paper really brought back some memories.

Jeff put the receipt up to his nose and sniffed at it. Then, holding the receipt between both hands, he rolled his thumbs around feeling its texture.

Eventually, Jeff fell asleep on his couch while holding the receipt clinched tightly in his grasp.

He slept soundly till early dawn.

As Jeff awoke his cell phone rang. It was his default ringtone and said: *Unknown* on the caller ID. Jeff generally ignored such phone calls. However, something told him to answer it this time.

He went with his conscience for he had a superior conscience.

He answered using his phone voice. He said, "Hello."

The lady on the other end identified herself as Kim, an RN at the Rappaport Medical Center. Already Jeff was weighed down with uneasiness. Therefore, Jeff's voice changed back to its original tone with an additional tremble. "Okay," Jeff spoke abruptly as the lady paused to take a breath.

"Are you Jeff Roberts?"

"Yes. What's wrong?"

"Is your wife Linda?"

Jeff's throat swelled with worry as his heartbeat switched patterns from the anxiety he was experiencing. He gulped and felt as if he swallowed a gigantic meatball. "Yes."

"Is there any way you can make it up here? It is important. I have something to discuss with you and it has to be done in private according to HIPAA laws."

"Just tell me. Is she okay?"

"It's not the best news. But there is some optimism."

"What do you mean? Is she okay or not?" Jeff became riddled with emotion. His nostrils flared as a huge vein formed on his forehead. He needed to know something. Anything was better than nothing. If it was bad news he needed to know. There was no way he could drive sixty miles worrying and not knowing of Linda's condition. He would continue to speak expelling tremendous concern through his vocal cords until the nurse, finally, told him something to trim the fret.

"I need to see you in private."

"Just tell me what happened to her. I can't drive that long of a distance, worried sick, not knowing what is wrong with her. C'mon! I need to know some—" Jeff was really getting himself worked up. However, his emotional spill was effective.

The nurse went against the rules. Lowering her voice, she said, "She was in a car wreck."

Suddenly, Jeff's mind entered a black void. He was solemn.

Chapter Fourteen

Rappaport, IL

September 3rd, 2005

(A year and two days after Jeff and Linda wedded)

The prison yards and corridors were filled with slipshod inmates—men in bright orange jumpsuits. Voices resonated—sharp sailor tongues. The concrete was damp and gray and merged into ice cold steel bars. The bars were so cold they displayed a tinge of blue.

You may have heard of a place called Alcatraz. Picture, if you will, the exact same place but on complete land.

What makes this prison compare to such a historic monument? It was once an insane asylum—better yet, an infirmary. It closed down for many years and was even reported as haunted before a man by the name of Leonard Buxton bought it and turned it into a maximum security prison. In fact, with no name being given to it, that's what it became known as— Buxton House of Corrections. Or as the locals called it: Hell Cell.

Leonard Buxton lived outside of Rappaport and never entered the town. He had a personal vendetta over a failed attempt to recover the stock exchange. He was eventually accused of laundering money and held a grudge against the whole town. His nefarious plot was to have arrested those who wronged him so he could assure them they'd be treated like pigs. For a while, he was a man of great power.

However, from Central City to Dover, the prison became a reservoir for murderers and rapists.

It overlooked a scenic view. And it was in a beautiful location with acres and acres of land for the inmates' curriculum. It was just the stuff that went on inside the dungeon that produced the horror that occurred.

Of these inmates was the infamous Lullaby Killer. However, I mentioned him earlier as Jack Rebus. "Lullaby Killer" was his media-given pseudonym. Just as Charles Manson was known as Helter Skelter, Ed Gein was known as the Butcher of Plainfield, and David Berkowitz was known as Son of Sam, Jack Rebus was the Lullaby Killer.

As Jeff Roberts phrased it on a recording while gathering information for a novel he attempted to write:

"He would relax his victims with a soothing voice and massages, putting them into a hypnotic-like state. Then, with the power of manipulation, he would coax them into taking their own lives. He preferred the method of hanging due to his fascination with executions. When he was finished he would clean up the crime scene and position them to look as if they died in their sleep."

Speaking of which, on the day before the execution Jack was paid a visit. It was a lanky fellow dressed in a navy blue police officer uniform. He was led to an interrogation room where the monster waited. The monster being Jack Rebus.

The man introduced himself as Officer Jeff Roberts.

Jeff explained to Jack the reason for his visit. He said, "I have decided to write a novel, a true crime genre, based on your life as a serial killer. I only have an hour for the interview so I need to ask the most important questions. Would you be willing to cooperate?"

Jack snarled, "Yes," followed by a hiss.

"Okay. Then, let's begin," Jeff said as he set up his audio recording equipment. He wasn't allowed to bring in video recording equipment. That was fine. All he needed was audio.

Jeff began the session—a familiar conversation: "Why did you kill? What made you kill?"

"Power. Control. Envy. Lust." Jack gave a variety of simple answers and grinned sadistically between each word.

"What was your weapon of choice? I mean, the papers said you killed them by strangulation. Did you ever use any weapons other than your bare hands?"

"Cop, do you believe everything you hear? They killed themselves. I was the little voice inside their heads."

"Did you ever feel regret?"

"Regret means you're sorry. It shows weakness. I am not weak nor am I sorry."

"What made you want to kill?"

Jack turned to Jeff with a gleam in his eye grinned sadistically and said, "You."

"What do you mean?"

"You are the voice I hear every time I…." Jack paused. "Don't refer to it as kill. I simply sacrifice. A life is meant to be taken as well as lived. You'll see. You'll soon see."

"So you got pleasure out of—?"

"I have never felt pleasure." Jack changed the subject. "How's that pretty little wife of yours?"

"This interview is over."

Jeff stood up and walked off.

He was terrified inside but refused to show it on the outside. And as he walked away he never looked back. However, he was urged to. Something kept telling him to. He felt static behind him as if a powerful force attempted to take possession of his soul. Jeff knew that Jack was watching him with that evil, distant stare.

He had the devil's eyes.

There was no soul in them.

Jack needed a soul.

Chapter Fifteen

Dover, IL

September 1ˢᵗ, 2004

(A year and two days before the interview with Jack Rebus)

The blustery winds exhaled in numbers. The lights dimmed inside a small white house. Inside the house sat Jeff Roberts by a lamp with his lap beneath a desk. He pounded the characters on his keyboard as words came together on his monitor.

With a mess of information together Jeff tried to condense it together to construct a plot worth giving interest to.

It was clearly relevant that Jeff was near the point of entering follies. He wanted so badly to get inside the mind of Jack Rebus. He would act out forming his own dramatizations to include credible detail in his draft. And by doing this he became so caught up in embellishment that his work was developing a fictitious plot rather than biographical persuasion.

On the whole, Jeff was getting too caught up in the novel.

He decided to take a break.

Jeff entered Marty's GameRoom. It said so on the flashy marquee overhead.

He approached the bar slowly.

He ordered two shots of whiskey. He told the bartender to make it a double but in separate glasses. He downed both of them back to back as if he chased one with the other.

Jeff was in high spirits and ready to tie one on.

A few feet from him, at a singles' table, sat a beautiful young woman. She watched Jeff closely as he glanced at her in fidgets. He was shy moreover than her. She acted not the slightest bit coy.

He was urged by his conscience to make his move, however, nervous. He wasn't quite bullet proof yet. A few more shots of bourbon and he would win his prize. So, he thought.

"Another," he would say to the bartender. He did this several times before "Another" turned into "Anudder".

There he was—a sloppy mess.

He could barely stand but defied the laws of gravity. His gate was horrible. His legs wobbled. He was definitely feeling the effects.

He approached her abruptly. However, she found him to be whimsical.

He said to her, "You come here often?" His words were scrunched together and trampled over one another. Plus, he belched afterward.

She covered her mouth daintily. It was uncertain for what reason. It could've been the avoidance of inhaling his nasty breath. Or, it could've been to hide her laughter. It didn't matter. There was something about him that fascinated her and she was intrigued to find out more.

He eventually grabbed a chair from another table and sat down next to her.

They talked for hours.

He introduced himself as Jeff, through his drunken speech, and she reciprocated.

She said, "My name is Linda, Linda Duple." Her voice was soft and beautiful—sheer elegance.

She asked him for his last name.

He hesitated at first, almost as if he had forgotten, but, then, he replied, "Roberts. I'm a cop," and, then, smiled from ear to ear as if his occupation was relevant to the question.

For Linda that was like the icing on the cake. Her eyes lit up with fires of passion at that very moment.

They still continued to talk. They stayed till close and got to know each other very well. Jeff had such a great time and was so involved with her company. He sobered up within a couple of hours of conversation.

Later that night, they communed at his place. Jeff told her about his fascination with Jack Rebus and about the book he was writing, or trying to write. Linda was very excited to hear all about it.

It's funny how destiny works. Neither one of them was aware, at that moment, of their commitment to one another. Linda looked deeply into Jeff's eyes and saw an eternity.

Jeff turned his radio on and tuned into his favorite station—101.1 FM *The Wire*. The song that played was: When I Look into Your Eyes by Firehouse. It wasn't long before the two were undressed and making love.

That very moment changed Jeff's life forever. He retired his book idea. Nonetheless, he strived for a promotion at the station. And at Linda's will he gave up drinking. A year later, they got married.

Chapter Sixteen

Rappaport, IL

September 5th, 2005

Jack was ready to walk the green mile. In fact, the executioner's song played in his mind on a loop. He feared neither death nor captivity but did, however, fear freedom and the vices of those who wished him dead—the loathers.

There was no remorse.

Heaven wouldn't have him and Hell couldn't hold him. He had no salvation and knew that damnation would be the pit of his wretched ghost.

It was the day. There was nothing else to do besides sit and wait. And he craved the drug. He hungered for the trio of chemicals that would flush through his veins and squeeze his heart till it stopped beating.

Suddenly, the priest entered. With a wet cloth, he cleansed Jack's brow. He said, "Are you ready, my son? Are you ready to be handed your judgment by God Almighty?" Jack replied with a weary nod.

However, he said with thin lips through gnashed teeth, "There is no God."

As the priest exited the cell, with a wayward Jack trailing behind, he read scripture from his bible. It was Psalm 23. Aloud, he read, "The Lord is my shepherd I shall not want. He makes me lie down in green pastures. He leads me beside still waters. He restores my soul. He leads me in paths of righteousness for his name's sake. Even though I walk through the valley of the shadow of death I fear no evil for you are with me. Your rod and your staff, they comfort me. Surely goodness and mercy shall follow me all the days of my life; and I shall dwell in the house of the Lord forever. Amen."

Jack looked beyond a glass window that encased an audience. There were well over a hundred people crammed tightly in the room that waited for Jack to breathe his last breath.

There were three executioners. They assisted Jack upon a cushioned table. They fastened leather straps around his forearms. They explained to him that euthanasia can burn and has been known to cause fits. He looked on. Unthreatened.

He could feel the penetration. The sound the needle made as it entered his tough flesh and penetrated his vein was a loud pop. And just as one could imagine being sedated for surgery it was lights out. The euthanasia was painless.

He lay lifeless with a pleasant smile.

Jack's time of death was exactly 2:30 PM.

Immediately family and friends of those who were victimized by Jack felt a huge weight lifted from their chests. They loathed that man and even Linda Sue (it said so on her name badge), who had firm beliefs that it was wrong to take a life under any circumstance, smiled from ear to ear as she watched him perish. She said between her teeth, "An eye for an eye. A tooth for a tooth." Then, she said with stronger emotion, "Go to hell where you belong, you monster!"

Buxton House of Corrections was one inmate less.

The execution was even broadcasted on live television. Channel five. It was even re-aired on 5@5 (a news program that aired on channel five at five o'clock).

It became a media circus. There were online forums created, blogs written, and even a webpage (www.jackrebus-execution.trd) built by a group of teens with way too much time on their hands that only consisted of a VEVO player that comprised his execution.

To prove how sick people are the webpage acquired over a thousand hits the first week it was up and running.

No one mourned the loss. Jack was heartless. A coldblooded killer. He preyed on people's vulnerabilities and insecurities.

It is engraved on his tombstone: BETTER OFF DEAD.

That was Buxton's last execution before the prison was forced to shut down in 2008.

Chapter Seventeen

Dover, IL

September 5th, 2005

The same day as Jack's execution Jeff was rushed to the ER. A coincidence, perhaps, but in no way connected.

It was exactly 2:30 PM when Jeff was grazed with a bullet and knocked out cold. His partner, at the time, thought Jeff had been shot in the head. There was blood present, however, not enough to represent a fatal wound.

His partner panicked and rushed him to the closest hospital while screaming: "Officer down! Officer down!" into his radio.

Linda was in hysterics when she found out.

She illustrated her concern unmistakably.

She had already decided she loved Jeff. He felt the same.

Jeff had a dubitable nightmare while he was unconscious. And he had never been one to dream. However, this was more than a dream. It was almost as if Jack Rebus was trying to contact him.

Jeff explicated, with vivid detail, his mental excursion to Linda. And he swore to never tell another soul for as long as he lived.

It all started from within the prison walls. Jeff was walking down a dimly lit corridor. He even remembered the outfit he wore. His choice of clothing made the dream that much stranger. Jeff had never worn such an ensemble. He wore a yellow polo shirt, with the crocodile logo sewn above the pocket, and a pair of tan corduroy pants that were threadbare in a few spots.

In any case, every cell contained an inmate.

As he walked past the inmates said his name. The voices all sounded alike and eventually created a reverb. Then, just before he came to, he realized something. Every inmate was Jack Rebus. As Jeff's dream ended he heard a soft angelic voice singing Brahm's Lullaby. As he awoke the song crossfaded into a mother singing to her baby outside his room.

He jolted. Covered in sweat.

Linda was pleased to know Jeff's wound was nothing more than a graze rather than a hole. However, he was disoriented. Quickly Linda leapt to his side and assured him that everything was okay. She explained to him the accident. It was then, he elucidated to Linda his nightmare.

Jeff thought hard about the outfit he wore in his dream. He remembered seeing it somewhere before. Then, it came to him. He recalled himself, with fixed eyes, looking at a photo. He studied it hard. It was the first photo he had ever seen of Jack Rebus. It was in a scrapbook in the courthouse exhibit room. Jack was a child in the photo. He wore the exact outfit. Cold chills went up and down his spine.

What did all of this mean? Jeff truly felt like he was losing his sanity. But still, Linda held on. She had no clue as to the demons he was battling. She only saw what everyone else saw—actuality.

Jeff being shot startled her into thinking he was gone forever. Now she realized her strength of devotion.

That very moment attested to Linda's love for Jeff. She absolutely refused to leave his side. She held onto him tightly.

He loved the attention.

Later that night, the two of them watched an Alfred Hitchcock marathon. Jeff was still in the hospital and Linda decided to stay overnight with him. He explained to her that she didn't have to stay and that she was free to go home anytime. She insisted.

Jeff learned quickly that she was a stubborn woman—beautiful, but stubborn.

Jeff's head was bandaged as you see in old army movies. It was only a flesh wound and just caused him minor pain. And the only reason he was admitted was for continuous observation. The doctor was concerned about him arriving unconscious moreover than the wound itself—a neurological thing.

Linda kissed Jeff on the lips. It was a passionate kiss with seductive persuasion. It was apparent that Linda wanted to make love. Jeff knew this and didn't hesitate one bit.

He reached over her, grabbed hold of the privacy curtain, and pulled it to.

March of the Marionettes played in the background as the television flashed brightness—a slow strobe. Their silhouettes were etched upon the curtain and moved in erotic forms.

It didn't take Linda long to climax. The thrill of taking a risk overly aroused her. And as for Jeff…the coitus was the best ever.

She quivered and twitched which sent him into overdrive.

Chapter Eighteen

The Demise of Granny Picket

Darkness mixed with fear can create an anxiety that fabricates exaggeration upon a protruding animate force.

She lay on her couch calling out, "Whiskers. Where are you, kitty? Come to Momma." With no response from her cat, she stood upright, with a slight curve in her posture, and went to look for her pet.

She went outside.

It was a beautiful night. The moon was brightly lit and filled the sky with a ghostly fluorescence. She became slightly mesmerized by this. However, she was quickly reminded by a tattered ball of yarn on her porch to look for her kitty.

She searched high and low calling for her once more, "Whiskers. Where are you, kitty?" She had no luck.

Meanwhile, a silhouette entered the back door. It was the shape of a man—big and stalwart. He held something in his hand. He crept eerily through the void of his existence. Who was he and what was his purpose?

Soon…Granny Picket decided to give up her search for Whiskers. Also, she felt a bit sleepy. She entered her home and headed straight for the couch. That's where she slept most of the time.

Carefully she sat down and, then, positioned herself comfortably. It wasn't before long she was sound asleep.

Later, as she rested, the shadowy figure skulked over her. He breathed heavily with a distinctive sigh every other exhale. He held a mysterious object. He moved it into better focus revealing that it was a thick strand of rope. It appeared to measure twelve inches in length.

He wasn't there to play games.

It was pure vendetta.

And he didn't waste any time.

He wrapped the rope around her neck, lifting her fragile head, and wrenched the rope till the life drained out of her. But it wasn't as simple as he imagined. Granny Picket put up a fight. She grabbed at the behemoth, prying her fingers between the rope and her neck. She kicked and squirmed with violent twists. But that's all she could do. Sadly it wasn't long before her body's reaction ceased.

Granny Picket was dead.

There stood the shadowy figure.

He knew his actions would be questioned. Therefore, he had to come up with a quick plan. He considered disposing of the body. However, that had been proven as flawed judgment over the years.

He thought long and hard.

He was in no hurry to leave.

Nobody ever paid the poor woman a visit.

He needed to come up with a clever way of hiding his violent doings. Suddenly, it came to him. He would simply fix her to appear as though she died in her sleep. She was an old woman, nevertheless.

The killer neglected to consider, however, a crucial piece of evidence—the markings on her neck where she had been strangulated. There was no covering that up.

He did clean up before he left. He didn't want to make it appear as though there had been a struggle, although, most of the struggle was on the couch. Therefore, a few items were displaced and scattered on the floor before the couch.

The killer neatly arranged everything that had fallen or was knocked out of place back into order.

Soon, with no sense of remorse or acknowledgment of his brutal renderings, he exited the house with a pleasant gate.

Chapter Nineteen

The Present

1

The obituary read:

Grace "Granny" Sue Picket

A memorial service will be held August 12 for Granny Picket who was found deceased at her residence August 8. Cause of death is yet unknown. She was 87.

Picket was born on February 3, 1923, in Mueller Tennessee to Claire and Joseph Picket. She was never married and has no known children. She resided in Dover, Illinois in 1993.

She lived her life as a homemaker and enjoyed the company of her cat Whiskers.

Memorial contributions may be made to the First Church of God in Dover to the Friends of Westminster Commune in care of the Give to Live Foundation.

2

Jeff sat outside Linda's room in a waiting area.

On his way to the hospital, the car practically drove itself. Jeff was aloof. However, he did come to once he entered the driveway. And instantly reality hit him. Linda was in there, somewhere, badly injured. Oh, my God,

Jeff thought. Would she be mangled? Would her head be split open and held together by some medical device? Would she be in a state of vegetation? Would she be missing an appendage or two—an arm, a leg? These were questions that flourished in Jeff's mind.

In his six years of law enforcement, Jeff had seen it all. Yet he wasn't prepared for what he was about to walk into. And being that he was unaware of her overall condition it bothered Jeff that much more.

The RN he had spoken to earlier over the phone met him at the central nurses' station. Her name was Kim. She slowly walked with Jeff to Linda's room slightly ahead to guide him. And as they walked she explained to Jeff Linda's condition. Of course, it was all in medical jargon. Jeff looked confused so Kim started all over repeating it all in laymen's terms.

It was not good. In summary, she explained to Jeff that Linda was in a coma and could take up to ten years, if not more, to come out of. Jeff broke down in the middle of the hallway. He didn't want to hear that.

He requested to see Linda's doctor.

The nurse assured him he would have his chance to speak to the doctor later. She said, "For now, I'll give you some time alone with her. The doctor may be in later to check on her. You can speak to him then."

Just then, Jeff realized he was standing on the threshold of his beloved's room. He looked up and saw her lying there. She was still amongst the living but lay motionless as if she was dead. Practically every inch of her body was bandaged. In addition, she had tubes galore coming out of her body—each one connected to some contraption. This, of course, filled Jeff with doubt. Much doubt.

3

In Dover Dale was getting along wonderfully. He was released from the hospital. He had returned to work, however, with restricted duties. In précis, he would dispatch till the doctor said otherwise. Dale hated to hear that.

When Dale was informed of Jeff's whereabouts and his reason for being he was drained of all happiness. Dale thought a lot of Linda. In fact, Jeff and Linda were nearly like his kinfolk. He considered them to be anyway.

And Dale wanted to see her badly. He figured Jeff could use a friend about now. However, he had already lost a lot of work time and needed to make up for it. Besides, the investigation concerning Granny Picket's death was current and Dale was committed to his job. He assured himself that he would see Linda soon.

With Jeff being gone on a family medical leave they needed all the manpower they could get. Although Dale didn't feel like much help—dispatching—he relieved the original dispatcher so he could work the beat in Dale's place.

4

With gentle fingers, Jeff stroked Linda's cheek. It was the only bare spot on her face. He wanted her to feel his touch against her nude flesh in hopes she would respond to it. As stated earlier: *a woman knows her lover's touch*. She didn't respond. Her comatose state was too severe.

Jeff refused to leave Linda's bedside. He held to her a promise. He swore he would always be there for her. Now was the time to prove it. He lost a lot of sleep and weight.

It was going on day four and Jeff was ten pounds lighter than he was before he arrived at the hospital. Jeff needed a good hot meal. He needed a shower. Most importantly he needed a good twelve-hour sleep. However, he was miserable, jaded, and heartsick.

5

Dale decided to take a break from dispatching and go see Linda. He knew that Jeff was still at the hospital and could probably use some comforting.

His arm was still bandaged and aloft in a sling. He didn't let that affect his driving abilities albeit told not to. Those were the strictest of orders from his doctor: "Do not drive!" Dale's ethics of compliancy were poor.

Sixty miles is well over an hour and a half long drive. But Dale would make it in forty-five minutes, at most.

6

Jeff stepped out long enough to get him some coffee.

While in the break room, where all the vending machines were, Jeff overheard a conversation. The voices were of male and female gender. They sounded as if they were in the same boat as him. But, then, Jeff heard a third voice. It was a doctor. The male and female were told to step into a room. The news wasn't good. Suddenly, Jeff heard ebullition. Firstly, the female voice blasted out. Secondly, the male voice joined. From that Jeff produced the theory that there must've been a death.

Immediately Jeff rushed to Linda's room.

As he entered the threshold he saw Dale. They crashed into each other wrapping arms around one another's bodies. They squeezed each other tightly with desperation.

They sat down—Jeff on the side of Linda's bed and Dale in a chair he pulled closer. Jeff explained to Dale her condition. Dale was equally affected. How could this be? And as the two of them discussed Linda's chance of survival the conversation took a turn.

Jeff already knew about Granny Picket. Dale informed him of the investigation's progress and how McDermott, a second-ranked investigator, didn't know his ass from a hole in the ground. Then, the conversation took another turn.

"You have lost a lot of weight," said Dale.

"I've not had an appetite. Been too down," replied Jeff.

Then, Dale noticed the black rings around Jeff's eyes not to mention the bags beneath them. "Have you not slept? You look like you're on a week-long drunk."

"Can't sleep either."

"Go home, Jeff. I understand your pain but you have to keep your own strength up, man."

"I can't leave her."

"Jeff, she'll be fine. You can still come to see her. The nurses. The doctor. They'll keep you informed of any changes in her condition. Come on. You're killing yourself."

Dale had a point and he touched a nerve. Jeff was aware of this and even concurred. Therefore, he kissed Linda upon her bandaged lips and with tear-filled eyes said, "I'll never leave you. I love you way too much."

Chapter Twenty

Dale's presence was complete solace to Jeff. Just Dale being near gave Jeff the strength to move forward. And he did.

Jeff was back at home and at work. Dover needed a lead investigator that knew what he was doing rather than McDermott…who didn't. And if that wasn't enough Dale was fully recuperated and ready to resume his regular position as a police officer—working the beat.

There they were—a modern day Batman and Robin.

Albeit Jeff was concerned about Linda he fooled others to believe he wasn't affected the least bit. Jeff was never one to wear his heart on his sleeve. Dale knew this. Therefore, Dale would explain to the others that Jeff was affected.

Dale respected Jeff and didn't want the others to go on thinking Jeff cared nothing about his beloved Linda.

That was far from the truth.

The current investigation was Granny Picket's suspicious death. They all agreed on homicide, however, had no leads. And the longer Jeff thought about it he found it more and more similar to a Jack Rebus killing.

The citizens of Dover thought they were safe ever since Jack Rebus was executed. Therefore, a town meeting was held. Only important figures were asked to attend.

At the meeting, they discussed many things affiliated with Granny Picket's death. However, one thing they agreed on was to keep all accusations of homicide and "whodunits" away from the media's attention. This would prevent panic and fear. If anyone was to ask what happened to Granny Picket, "She died in her sleep," would be the most suitable reply.

Jeff and Dale knew better. They knew her death wasn't natural. Therefore, they would have to investigate discreetly in hopes that soon an apprehension would be made. But when Jeff and Dale united forces it was like a combination of CHiPs meets Laurel and Hardy.

Discreet would not be easy.

They would wait till nightfall to conduct their investigations. They were told not to question anyone until further notice. Dale would make wisecracks, such as: "How the hell can someone investigate a crime without asking folks questions?"

In return, Jeff would reply: "Elementary, my dear Watson. Elementary." That was a touch of humor used to defuse Dale's "wannabe" temper. It worked.

Dale was a docile thing. Very meek. Watching him lose his temper was entertaining. It was as if he was putting on a show.

Jeff loved to get him riled up.

During all of this, Jeff was battling his own demons—fighting off emotions.

While he worked he would do everything he could to take his mind off Linda. It wasn't easy. And if the mere thought of her lying in that hospital bed crossed his mind he would break down immediately—losing all sense of equanimity. He didn't care where he was or who saw him.

But as mentioned earlier, Jeff wasn't one to wear his heart on his sleeve.

He did the best he could at maintaining his composure.

Dale, on the other hand, was affected, likewise. He too cared for Linda. But after all, it was easier for him to carry on less distraught.

When Jeff was alone he was a complete mess.

Dale found the situation worrisome, however, was more optimistic than Jeff.

But beyond the rise of concern for Linda, they had an investigation to undergo.

They would park the Explorer in an unobserved location down at the bottoms.

The "bottoms" is where the old reservoir was. Teenagers used to party and act carelessly down there. However, Dale put an end to that during his first week as a cop. That's another story.

Beyond the darkness, with only a flashlight to guide them, they would carefully snoop around. Also, they would dust objects for fingerprints.

They did this for three weeks straight.

The only prints that showed up were Jeff's. He claimed to have been sloppy the night he found Granny Picket dead. Other than that they had nothing they could use.

On the other hand, Dale did notice something. It was something that created suspicion. It wasn't in Granny Picket's yard. At that, this only added to his suspect of interest—Curtis Blackwell.

The whole time, since Granny Picket's untimely death, Dale accused one person. He never spoke of this. However, he dwelled on the idea. And maybe, being that he already thought hard about the possibility, seeing the object gave him the chance to make true of his judgment.

Without a moment's hesitation, Dale said to Jeff, "Hey! Look over there in Curtis's yard. Near his porch. What do ya see?" It was dark and Dale shined the flashlight over so Jeff could take a gander. How Dale saw it in the first place was beyond disbelief. He had to have been focusing hard—glancing over at Curtis's yard ever so often to have seen it.

They walked over and stared down at the object—Dale, of course, leading the way. It was a twelve-inch rope. It just lay on the ground with no purpose. Simultaneously Jeff and Dale turned to one another. They locked eyes and their expression said it all.

Chapter Twenty-one

"Think about it, Jeff. When we destroyed his rose bush, leading him to believe that Granny Picket did it, it fucked his mind up, man," explained Dale.

"I can't see Curtis doing that. He's not a killer," Jeff replied.

"That's all we got, man. I mean, the dude has a motive."

"That would make us involved," Jeff spoke with a grave tone.

57

"How's that?"

"Dale, if he killed her over his roses that means we set him off in the first place. It's all our fault."

"No! Not true! It was a harmless diversion. He killed her because he's a sick motherfucker."

"I guess this gives us a lot to think about then." Jeff ended the conversation.

They sat in his office and tossed around ideas, speculations, and theories. Dale wanted Curtis to be the killer all this time. However, Jeff needed more evidence to be convinced. That put them in a tough spot. They felt as if they reached a plateau in their investigation. They were given orders from headquarters to not question anyone. They found a suspect. Now they needed to interrogate him.

Unfortunately, for Dale, he minded his police chief with deference.

However, Jeff didn't give a damn.

He took orders from nobody.

He was a firebrand.

Jeff said, "Let's go get 'em."

Dale strongly opposed by saying, "Chief Wilkins will have my badge! Fuck you! I'm staying right here!"

On their way to Curtis Blackwell's Dale sat quietly and sullenly.

Jeff said, "Cheer up, buttercup."

Dale replied in an arch tone, "You can kiss my ass!" Then, his tone changed to a vexed quality as he added, "I'm dead. So fucking dead. And it's your fault."

"Do you want me to stop the car and let you out? It's all you, bro. All ya gotta do is fucking say it!" Jeff spat in angst.

Dale drew back and reposed, "If I lose my job can I come and work strictly for you?"

Jeff giggled at Dale's puppy dog expression and acted as if he was going to concur. However, he looked at Dale with a moment of serious conduct and said, "Hell no!"

58

They both laughed. That was their humorous conduct.

Jeff pulled into Curtis Blackwell's driveway. He and Dale wasted no time at exiting the vehicle. Once they entered the gate it was straight forward. And Beyond the gate, they stood staring at the house most people feared.

Jeff flashed a folded piece of paper at Dale. "What's that?"

"A search warrant saying we can enter his house without prior approval."

"How the hell'd ya get that?"

"The internet. Ya ever been there?"

Dale lowered his head and lightly shook it.

Jeff shrugged his shoulders and chuckled, "What?"

"Are you serious?"

"As a heart attack."

"We're in so much trouble."

Jeff had never seen Dale act so worried. But Jeff wasn't about to shift gears. Their mission was to get Curtis out of that house even if it meant going in and dragging him out by the collar.

They knew he was in there.

Jeff knocked on the front door as Dale knocked on the back door. Jeff yelled, "I'll give you three seconds to come out." As he pounded loudly he yelled, "If you're not out in three I have a warrant that says I can come in." Jeff gave Curtis a brief moment to heed his warning. "One. Two." Before Jeff could finish the door flung open. And beyond the door's threshold stood the eerie behemoth Curtis Blackwell.

In avoidance of Dale losing his job, Jeff decided to conduct the interrogation at Curtis's house. Therefore, they could look around and gather more evidence while they were there.

Dale was all for the idea.

On the other hand, Curtis wasn't too cooperative. He explained to Jeff that he knew about Granny's death. However, he knew nothing of the cause.

Jeff spoke to Curtis till he was blue in the face. He refused to leave until either a confession was made or Dale found crucial evidence. Neither Dale nor Jeff had any luck. Either Curtis wore an impenetrable disguise or he was telling the truth. Eventually, Jeff and Dale grew tired. That being said they gave it a rest and called it a night.

Chapter Twenty-two

The shadowy behemoth appeared again. This time not as large. However, his silhouette was the same.

He stood stoutly on the porch of an unfamiliar residence as if he awaited the occupant's exile.

Meanwhile, in the house, a young woman wearing panties and a long t-shirt pulled a pair of pants from her dryer. She pressed the denim against her nude arms realizing the dampness. "Fuck it," she said as she put them on.

She walked through the entrance hall and stood at the aperture of the stairwell. She yelled, "I'm going out to the car, Robert. I think I left the keys in the ignition." Her voice echoed and resonated up the stairs. There was, however, no reply.

The young woman stormed out the door and to her car which was parked beneath an aluminum carport. The shadow of the killer was gone. However, he waited in the bushes—anxious to attack.

The young woman found her keys but dropped them with clumsy fingers. She bent down to pick them up and as she stood upright the figure reappeared...behind her.

In the course of his attack, a muffled scream was exhaled but failed to be heard.

Jeff awoke with a massive migraine—the kind he used to experience after long nights of drinking hard liquor. He didn't go out drinking the night before. However, the pain was dour.

Jeff rolled over and extended his arm toward his bedside table until he touched the surface. He felt blindly for his bottle of pills. Maybe Tylenol. Perhaps Motrin. Once he found the pills he quickly snatched them from where they sat and twisted off the cap. The safety seal popped noisily. He sat in the semi-fowler's position just long enough to consume the medicine.

At that, he didn't take just one or two. He put the bottle up to his lips and tipped it over. Then, he crunched them in his mouth as he chewed. When Jeff was done devouring the pills he took a sip of stale water which also sat on his bedside table in a huge Styrofoam cup. He rested his head in a soothing position, relaxed his eyelids, and waited for the pain to subside. Before too long he began to drift back to sleep.

He had no recollection of the entire night. Therefore, he must've slept soundly. Yet he felt as if he hadn't slept at all. Maybe it was the migraine that exhausted him. Nonetheless, Jeff was under a lot of stress. Just as Jeff had succumbed to his exhaustion his cell phone rang. It was Bad Boys by Inner Circle which was Dale. He answered, "Hello?"

"Well. Good morning to you too, sunshine."

"What do you want?"

"You up and ready?"

"No."

"Well. Get dressed. I'm on my way ta pick you up in my new ride. It's a freaking Mustang. Two-thousand-ten. You gotta ride in this thing."

"I think I'll sleep in today. Goodbye," Jeff said as he ended the phone call. The phone fell from his frail grip as he became torpid. But, then, the phone rang again. Once more it was Dale. Restoring animation Jeff answered, "Yeah." This time he sounded slightly infuriated.

"You didn't let me finish."

"What is it?"

"We have another homicide."

That grabbed Jeff's attention and regenerated his body's energy. Morally excited he said, "Who is it?"

"I'm not certain of all the details. All I know is that it's a female. Police Chief wanted me to contact you. He wants you to check it out."

"Okay. Gimme five minutes. I'll be ready." Jeff tossed his phone aside and quickly got dressed.

Solving crimes was a thrill for Jeff—his nuance form of addiction. And every chance he got to put his skills to the test he became stimulated with anticipation.

He was like a kid in a candy store. Sure, a life was lost. But to Jeff, in a strange sense, it was a window of opportunity.

And ever since Jeff started his career in law enforcement nothing major had ever happened—for his sake. He saw a lot, true. But now his role as an investigator changed direction.

He was more involved these days.

Dale pulled into Jeff's driveway, honked his customized horn that sounded the first few recognizable notes of "Hawaii Five-0", and waited. Instantly Jeff appeared in the doorway—pixilated by his screen door.

He exited the house while slipping his arms through a short-sleeved, button-up, over-shirt. He stood on his porch and stared at Dale while slowly shaking his head in response to Dale's horn.

Dale yelled out, "Let's go. We can't keep our dead princess waiting."

Jeff replied as he trotted down the steps, "You're sick, man." And as he entered the passenger side of the vehicle he admired the interior. "Nice."

Dale reached beneath the console, grabbed a red and blue beacon light, plugged it into the empty orifice of his cigarette lighter, positioned it on his dashboard, and said, "Let's rock, amigo." He flipped the switch as red and blue lights swirled in synchronization.

Chapter Twenty-three

This time Jeff handled everything delicately as they made their way through the house. He avoided leaving his fingerprints on valuable evidence. He didn't want to make the same mistake twice.

Once more they dusted for fingerprints.

"What's goin' on?" asked Dale sounding concerned over the situation.

"I dunno. I just dunno," replied Jeff.

They both glanced at each other with intent.

Dale held a set of keys in his hand and dusted them. They lay near the victim.

"Dust 'em good. No tellin' how many people has handled them," instructed Jeff.

Jeff had not yet seen the body.

Suddenly Jeff noticed a familiar face out in the yard. It was Stedman. He was brown nosing around trying to get a story.

Jeff shook his head from side to side and went out to talk to him.

Jeff said, "Boy, what the hell are you doin'?"

Stedman replied with quivering lips, "I was sent down here. I heard there was a murder."

Immediately Jeff put his hand over Stedman's mouth. "Shhh. Shut the hell up. You're leaving right now. There was no murder. In fact, we're not even certain of the cause of death. But I tell ya now…there was no murder. Now leave." Stedman nearly pissed down both legs.

Jeff was effective.

Stedman left hurriedly.

Jeff remembered what Chief Wilkins had said: *Be discreet. Don't ask questions.*

If the wrong information fell into Stedman's hands the whole town would be in hysterics. Jeff couldn't let that happen.

Jeff went back inside.

Dale said, "Him again, huh?"

Jeff replied, "Yeah, but I got rid of him."

"You don't think he'll make up a story do ya?"

"I doubt it. I read his stuff. His writing sucks."

"Yeah, but you know how those reporters are. Always diggin' up something for a good story."

"I wouldn't worry." Jeff changed the subject. "Have you looked at the body?"

"Yeah. Poor thing. She looked like she was sleeping when she died." Jeff raised an eyebrow. Dale continued to speak, "You would think that. If it wasn't for the marks around her neck."

That's all Jeff needed to hear.

Dale's detective skills were poor. He only saw things as they were rather than looking outside the box.

Jeff knew right away that something wasn't right.   He asked Dale to repeat himself.

Dale said, "She looks like she's sleepin' over there. The position she's lying in is a sleeping-type position. But, Jeff, she has these huge marks around her neck. Like Granny Picket. Sure 'nuff. Looks like she's been strangled."

Still, Jeff wasn't sure he wanted to believe what he was hearing. He looked at Dale with a baffled expression. "I..." That's all Jeff could say. He was speechless.

Then, Dale said, "C'mon over here and look for yourself. You're the big shot."

Dale led Jeff to the body. It was covered up in a black tarp. Dale grabbed hold of the top end corner and jerked it off of her.

Jeff examined her thoroughly. He looked at Dale with a grave expression on his face and said, "Do you know what this means?"

Dale shrugged his shoulders. He had no clue. The best he could say was, "What?"

"Come here." Jeff wanted Dale to come closer. He didn't want the others to hear his theory. It was, however, no assumption. Once Jeff was able to speak softly and directly into Dale's ear he said, "We have another serial on the loose."

Dale looked at Jeff vaguely and said, "...killer?"

"Yeah, Dale. A serial killer. But that ain't all." Still, Jeff spoke softly. "It's a copycat."

Dale's eyes lit up like fire. Now he understood. He looked at Jeff and attested to his theory. He said, "Jack Rebus." He looked down at the body and added, "The Lullaby Killer."

Chapter Twenty-four

Dover, IL. Pop. 1798

At this point, Jeff was about to give up. He was exceedingly focused on solving the multiple homicide case, however, missed Linda. He was experiencing so much stress. He racked his brain, day in and day out, trying to figure out who the murderer was. Yet, he worried about Linda's recovery.

Jeff would wait for the perfect opportunity to pay Linda a visit. But for now, he couldn't abandon the case.

As for Dale, he was still concerned about his inability to shoot a man. He was already given the opportunity. However, he failed and wound up in the hospital for a week. His full recovery time took close to a month, albeit, he still experienced pain. But now things were picking up. They were solving a murder mystery and Dale wanted to be prepared. He refrained from bothering Jeff and took it upon his self to go out to Jeff's shooting range to conquer the fear.

And as for Jeff's headaches and sense of exhaustion, he came to a conclusion. He realized that every time he awoke with a migraine and fatigue another body was discovered. This became a trend. However, he brushed off the notion and didn't make much of it. Coincidences occur frequently. He convinced himself that stress was the foundation for his weary discomfort and nothing more.

Jeff sat quietly in his office reviewing possible evidence. There just wasn't enough. Hitherto, the case was like an unsolvable puzzle. But Jeff was as bold to believe that every mystery could be solved. He was just waiting for the right piece of evidence to fall into his lap. He needed some form of substantiation that would at least adhere to the crime being committed.

He sat for a moment in complete silence. His hands cupped with fingers locked upon his lap. He thought hard. Determined. Suddenly, he was told by his secretary over his speaker phone to pick up line one. And he did.

"Jeff Roberts. Clark's Detective Agency. How may I—?"

"Jeff, we need to talk."

Jeff knew that voice. It was his boss. And he sounded very angry. Smoothly Jeff said, "Okay. I'm all ears."

"No! In private. This afternoon." He spoke in fragments with chopped up messages. However, his meaning was delivered clearly.

"I'm s'posed ta meet with Dale and go over our—"

"Don't bother. Be in your office. I'll be there twelve sharp." Just then, a steady pulse was heard over the receiver.

This was enough to add to Jeff's stress. At this instant, Jeff felt as if he was at his breaking point.

What could be so important to discuss and at the same time infuriate his boss? Soon, Jeff would find out.

Jeff looked at his watch and saw that it was 10:57 AM. He picked up his phone and quickly dialed Dale's number. After two rings Dale answered, "Hello. It's Dale."

"Hey. It's Jeff. Cancel our appointment. We'll have to review our evidence later."

"Why?"

"I dunno. Boss man just called. He wants to talk to me around noon. He sounded pissed."

"What could you have done?"

"Not a clue."

"All right. Just call me later and tell me how it went."

"Will do."

"I gotta go, man. I'm getting ready to head into the station."

"All right. Talk later."

"Remember. Call me."

"I will. Okay. Gotta go."

The big hand landed on twelve. Just in perfect alignment with the little hand.

Jeff sat in his chair. His heart thumping and his palms were sweaty. By the tone of his boss's voice, he knew he was in trouble for something. But what?

Suddenly, Jeff's boss entered the door and it slammed behind him.

Meanwhile, Dale sat at his desk. He was about to take a big bite out of a sandwich when the phone rang. He answered the call and identified himself as Officer Dale Wilson at the Dover Police Department.

The voice on the other end was shaky. It sounded like an older female. Her purpose for calling was to give an anonymous tip. She stressed the fact that she wanted to remain anonymous. Therefore, by doing so, she refused to release her identity. Her claim was that she was a hundred percent certain that she saw Curtis Blackwell near the house on the day of the second murder. That was it. She hung up soon after she stated her claim. Dale did, however, attempt to call her back but she didn't answer her phone.

One thing bothered Dale. Curtis never left his house. However, this did add to Dale's suspicions. He wanted so badly to be right on this. But in criminal investigations, you can't accuse. You must be certain with concrete evidence.

Dale sat contently mulling over the call. Suddenly, his cell phone rang. It was Jeff.

Dale answered, "Talk to me."

Jeff didn't talk for the first few seconds. And when he did he sounded disconcerted. He said, "I got some horrible news. Actually, I got some good and bad news. Which do you want first?"

"I guess the bad."

"I've been taken off the case. The son of a bitch told me I was under too much stress to do the job."

"That's not fair. Something had to've made him come up with that."

"He said I was being too sloppy. Wilkins contacted him and told him that my prints were showing up everywhere. He said I was interfering more than helping. He gave me a week to get my shit together."

"Bummer, man. So what's the good news?"

"You've been appointed lead investigator during my suspension."

"I can't do this on my own."

"Well, I'm going to use this time to see Linda. I'm thinking about staying up there the whole week. You'll be fine. It's just a week."

Dale couldn't believe what he was hearing.

Once the phone conversation was over Dale set his cell phone down on the desk and developed a look of determination on his face. He grabbed a notepad, and a pen, and scribbled the name: *Curtis Blackwell.* Then, beside the semi-illegible name, he scribbled: *Lead Suspect.*

Chapter Twenty-five

Jeff pulled into the parking lot of the Rappaport Medical Center. He was pleased to be seeing Linda—yet, ashamed of the overall circumstances.

He didn't fret.

He walked into the hospital and was greeted by Kim, the RN. Immediately she quietly explained Linda's progress. She said, "She has yet to come out of the coma. But there's hope."

Jeff replied, "Hope is all I have left?"

"We need your correct number. One of our nurses said they tried to call you last night. A courtesy call. Someone by the name of Jack answered the phone. He was rather rude. They called the number a second time and no one answered."

"Odd. Did you dial the right number?"

"Michelle is here. She's the one who tried to get hold of you. Let's check."

They walked to the central nurses' station. "Michelle, sweetie, can you look up Jeff Roberts's number and confirm it please?"

"Sure can." Michelle thumbed through a notebook filled with numbers. "It is 555-680-2293."

Jeff grunted and said, "That's mine."

"Something must have been wrong with the satellite," said Kim making sense of the matter.

"Yup. Must've." Jeff looked at Kim and Michelle and shrugged his shoulders.

After the ordeal, Jeff went into Linda's room. Once more there she lay. Still, she was bandaged up.

Jeff, for a moment, eyeballed her fingers with high hopes of seeing them move. They didn't. Then, he walked over and kissed her on the forehead.

Jeff ached for certainty. He wanted nothing more than to see her make progress. Be it a mutter or a smile Jeff wanted to hear or see something.

As mentioned earlier Jeff felt as if the walls were closing in on him. Everything was falling apart. You can only bend so much before you snap in two and Jeff felt as if he was almost there. He needed something good in his life.

He kneeled beside Linda's bed and said a prayer.

As he was praying his cell phone rang. It was the default ringtone. Jeff stopped long enough to answer the call but hit *end* instead of *send*. He became frustrated—(mad at himself and all that surrounded him). He went into his call log and looked at his missed calls. The most recent call was listed as *Private*. However, Jeff saw something that grabbed his attention. A few calls down was a familiar number. It was one he had recently become very associated with. It was the number to the Rappaport Medical Center.

Jeff became curious. He looked at the number's date and time as it read October 3rd 11:07 PM. That was last night, Jeff thought.

Immediately Jeff related the date to an incident he was altogether familiar with. That was the same date as the second murder. Also, it was within the same timeframe as the assumed time of death. But that's just the way Jeff's mind worked. He treated everything as a conundrum.

Later that evening, Jeff sat in a chair with his head resting on the foot of Linda's bed. He held her hand in his.

He was awoken by a tap on the door. As he lifted his head he saw a lady in scrubs carrying a dozen roses jutting out of a vase. He stared perplexedly.

Carefully she set the roses down on her bedside table.

Once the lady exited the room Jeff walked over to the roses. There was a card attached to one of the stems by a thin string. Jeff tore the string from the stem and read the card.

On the card was written:

To Jeff's pretty little wife,

My sweet rosebud, you have blossomed. I watched you grow. But now your time is running low. You're worthless now, confined to a bed. Sleep an eternity. You're better off dead.

Yours 4-ever, Jack Rebus

In an instant, Jeff saw red.

Who could be so volatile as to send his helpless wife a threat?

Jeff related the entire message to Jack Rebus. It was signed by him and even branded Linda as "pretty little wife" the same as Jack did during the interview when Jeff was processing ideas for his novel. However, the whole presumption was redundant.

Jack was dead. There was no question about that. Hundreds of people watched him perish.

Then, who could it be?

The clockwork was turning in Jeff's puzzle-solving mind. Suddenly, his whole body tingled from the warm sensation of certainty.

He related the roses to Curtis Blackwell.

Jeff took the threat seriously. With all the murders occurring he refused to take any chances.

He had to think fast.

He called Amanda, Dale's sister, and asked if she wouldn't mind spending a couple of nights with Linda. Amanda consented with no questions asked.

Jeff put on a latex glove. He slid the vase of roses inside a giant Ziploc baggie—vigilant not to touch anything with his bare hands.

He stuck the card in his pant pocket. His only interest was to retrieve fingerprints from the vase, not the card, which he had already touched.

Subsequently, he sat and waited for Amanda to arrive.

At this point in time, he accused Curtis Blackwell. In spite of everything he had nothing to lose. And at that very moment, he turned professionalism into rage. His compliancy toward law no longer existed.

He was a vigilante.

Chapter Twenty-six

It was late. Dale had just tilted back in his recliner. He sprawled out like a bag of bones and pointed his remote toward the television set.

He surfed through the channels until he found his favorite station: Reality TV. Instantly he was content.

The show he was watching was a documentary about people living with split personalities.

Soon he was distracted by a series of pecks at his window. He looked and saw a silhouette. The outline appeared to be of a huge figure. Stalwart.

Dale panicked and experienced fear—the same kind of fear that Granny Picket experienced.

At first, he grabbed his gun that lay near in his holster.

He choked.

An expression of uncertainty stretched across his face.

He put down his gun and grabbed a baseball bat that rested against a nearby wall instead.

Slowly Dale walked up to his window to get a better view of the intruder. As he got closer the silhouette got smaller forming into the figure of a human presence of average size. Then, he was able to make out the intruder. He heaved a sigh of relief. It was only Jeff.

Dale rushed to his door, opened it, and welcomed Jeff to come inside. Jeff entered still holding the baggie with the vase of roses inside.

Once Jeff was inside they sat at Dale's kitchen table and confabbed. Dale was excited to see Jeff but also wondered why he wasn't in Rappaport with Linda. It wasn't long before Jeff explained.

"I think I know who the killer is. And there's my evidence." Jeff pointed at the baggie with the vase of roses inside.

"Where'd you get those?"

"From the hospital. They were sent to Linda. Right now your sister is with her. I had to bring you this evidence. Here…" Jeff reached into his pocket. He pulled out the card and handed it to Dale.

Dale read it aloud, "To Jeff's pretty little wife, my sweet rosebud, you have blossomed. I watched you grow. But now your time is running low. You're worthless now, confined to a bed. Sleep an eternity. You're better off dead. Yours forever, Jack Rebus." An expression of confidence consumed Dale's face. He looked at Jeff and said, "Give me that bag. Tomorrow I'll take it to the station and have the prints identified."

"Great!" Jeff was excited.

"I gotta ask. You sure you didn't touch this vase with your bare hands?"

"I'm a hundred percent certain. Dale, I used a latex glove."

"Okay. Hopefully, we can get some prints off here and case closed."

The two of them gave one another a high five.

Jeff went ahead and crashed at Dale's. He was already there. He didn't see any sense in driving home. Plus he was tired of sleeping in that cold and lonely house.

Dale fell asleep in his recliner and Jeff fell asleep on the couch. They were both worn out, stressed out, and worried for Linda's sake. Jeff, of course, was worried the most.

They both wanted to restore everything.

What happened?

They wanted everything to be the way it used to be. Before Linda's accident. Before the murders. It seemed as if Jeff entered a dark realm and pulled Dale along with him.

However, Dale did sleep soundly with the confidence that the killer would soon be identified.

As for Jeff, he wandered out the door leaving nothing but an imprint of his chassis on the couch.

His movements were steady and inattentive. Perhaps he was exhausted and decided during a period of consciousness that he needed some fresh air.

Chapter Twenty-seven

Linda lay stiffly. She was in an elongated state of slumber. Albeit she heard voices she could not respond. However, voices outside her room resonated with her ghost. It was the ghost that sat beside her. It yenned for the moment where it could lie inside of her and bring up with it Linda's physical state of being.

But that was the hope of it all.

The doctor would come in often and check on her. It wasn't that he anticipated a miracle. He just wanted to be there when a miracle occurred.

Linda's doctor described her condition as being brought on by traumatic brain injury. And on the Glasgow scale, which in relation to numerical degree measures the severity of one's comatose state, Linda was averred to be a 1.

Jeff awoke in his own bed. His shoes were caked in mud and his shirt was torn. Once more he had a migraine and felt exhausted.

There was a knock upon his door.

Jeff responded to the knock in his weary state. And after opening the door Jeff looked as if he was at sixes and sevens. "Dale…good morning," Jeff said confusedly.

"Where'd you go last night, man? I woke up and you were gone." Then, Dale looked down at Jeff's mucked shoes. "Gee, man. What's up with your shoes?"

"I dunno. I must've gone sleepwalking last night. What field or garden I walked through is beyond me." Jeff rubbed the back of his neck as he spoke.

"I just wanted to tell you, I'm taking the evidence and dropping it off at forensics." Dale noticed Jeff's puzzled gleam. "You know, the flowers and vase?" Then, Dale realized that Jeff wasn't acting like himself, however, refocused on his reason for being while ignoring Jeff's unusual displacement. "Hopefully, we should hear something soon."

Jeff responded vaguely, "Okay," as if he suddenly lost interest.

Dale left as Jeff still stood in complete lull.

Within a minute of Jeff's statuesque state of existence, he turned and walked back toward his bedroom.

His gate was zombielike.

The door slowly closed stopping at the jamb. A beam of sunlight seeped in through the doorsill casting a shadow's canvas upon the wall. In animation, a familiar figure walked amongst the receiving barrier.

Later that day, Dale was on his way back to Jeff's house. He was in his squad car. Something came across the radio: "Calling all cars to the Pinsky residence. A corpse has been discovered. All active and on-duty police officers must report immediately to the residence. The address is 104 Sycamore Drive."

"Damn," Dale said as he turned his car around and headed in the direction of the newest crime scene.

This would be Dale's first official case concerning a dead body without the assistance of Jeff.

Dale knew what to look for and did just that. The first thing he noticed was the position the body was lying in. Then, he noticed the markings around the victim's neck which indicated the possible cause of death.

The corpse was male.

Like the other gruesome discoveries the body was positioned as though it was in a torpid state, as well as strangulated.

This added to the others.

Now Dale was definitely concerned.

While outside, completing his investigation, Dale noticed a trail of footprints. Immediately he took his digital camera and snapped some shots.

Dale couldn't wait to tell Jeff about the discovery. Now he was even more anxious to go to Jeff's house.

Meanwhile, at the Rappaport Medical Center Linda still lay stiffly in her bed. The doctor was intercepted at the door by one of the nurses.

The miracle passed him by. Linda's ring finger twitched. Amanda had stepped out long enough to use the restroom so she missed it, as well.

Eventually, he entered her room and watched for a few minutes as he usually did. However, the one thing he had been waiting for was over in a flash.

Chapter Twenty-eight

It was dark out. Jeff sat at his kitchen table by a dim lamp. He browsed through the scrapbook that was marked: *Exhibit A.*

Lately, Jeff acted as if he had become obsessed with the contents of the scrapbook. It not only contained childhood pictures of Jack Rebus but photos of his poor defenseless victims, as well. Jeff's favorite was Macie Brown. She was found beneath a blanket with her head propped comfortably on a pillow. However, around her neck was the weapon. It was the only weapon Jack ever used—a rope.

Somewhere between his enjoyment and weary loss of focus, Jeff fell asleep.

He dreamed that he was at Macie's house watching Jack murder her—choking the life right out of her. Then, he appeared in Granny Picket's front room. She lay on her couch dead as Jeff stood over her with the rope in his hand. Then, he appeared at the top of a stairwell before a frightened man.

None of this made sense. But when he appeared at Linda's bedside, skulking over her with a rope in his hand, he awoke instantly frightened and confused. What did all of this mean?

When Jeff did awake he realized that it was daylight. The early morning sun glared through every window that Jeff had open.

Jeff decided that he needed some fresh air.

While outside on his veranda he took out his cell phone and called the Rappaport Medical Center. When a nurse answered the phone, without delay, Jeff asked about Linda. The nurse put him on hold only to return within minutes with the same reply as always: "No miracles yet. But the doctor will contact you personally if anything good or bad does happen." It was as if they were reading from a script or teleprompter.

Jeff needed to hear something different.

Then, Jeff tried to contact Dale. He dialed Dale's number but an automated voice said, "This number has been changed or removed from our records."

Jeff thought out loud, "He didn't pay his bill. Guess I'll hop in the Explorer and go looking for him."

Dale had just returned to the station. Upon entering the door a fellow police officer stopped him. The policeman held a donut in one hand and a 12oz cup of coffee in the other. Also, he chewed on a bite he had just taken out of his donut. "Some whack job is here to see ya," the policeman said to Dale.

"Who is he?" Dale replied peering over the uniformed police officer's shoulder to catch a glimpse of the person.

"I dunno. He came in a little while ago. He's fidgety, out of breath, and he looks like he got into it with a freight train. We decided you could probably make sense out of his incoherent babble."

Dale approached the man with ease.

The man looked rough not to mention extremely frightened. Dale knew right away that the man had a story to tell.

The man stood outside Dale's office as Dale was able to carefully coax the man into following him. Circumspectly Dale shut the door behind them.

He seemed harmless.

"What's your name?" Dale asked in a cagy manner.

"Raw-Raw-Burt," the man replied with raspy breaths.

"Is it Burt?"

The man fiercely shook his head no.

"Take your time and…" Suddenly, Dale got an idea. He gave the man a sheet of paper and ink pen and said, "Here, write your name."

The man, with childlike penmanship, spelled out: R-O-B-E-R-T.

Dale read aloud, "Robert. Your name is Robert."

In Jeff's most recent vision, he stood before a frightened man at the top of a stairwell. It was the same man to which Dale spoke to now.

The man was so frightened for some mysterious reason. His ability to communicate was hindered.

Regardless of his inability to correspond Dale kept a close watch on him. In fact, he had him temporarily incarcerated just for protection. Dale knew that he held the key—the key to a chamber filled with vital information.

Chapter Twenty-nine

Dale was called into Chief Wilkins's office. A discovery was made, however, dreadful news for Dale. "Did we expel Jeff Roberts from our last investigation?" the Chief asked Dale.

"Yeah. Why?" Dale looked concerned, yet, anxious to hear the problem.

"And he's not been involved the entire time?"

"No. He's not. He's been in Rappaport. What are you hintin' at, Chief?"

"Prints came back."

"And…?"

"Jeff's prints are all over everything."

"There must be a mistake." Dale was in disbelief.

"Forensics don't lie, Dale." Chief Wilkins sounded confident.

"He must've interfered without anyone knowing. His wife is involved now, Chief. You know Jeff. He's stubborn as all get out. There has to be some logic behind this."

"Then, it's on you to get me the proof I need to get him off the hook. I'll give you twenty-four hours to bring me something. If I don't have any information releasing him as a prime suspect then… Dale, I have to go after him."

This lit a fire under Dale's ass.

Immediately Dale rushed to his squad car.

On his way over to Jeff's Dale entered a state of deep thought. So deep that upon entering Jeff's driveway he had no recollection of the trip. However, during the trip, his mind was adrift.

Dale reflected on Jeff's change of character. For a week straight Jeff had been acting strangely. At the time Dale considered it to be stress. However, his change of character evolved slowly and in sync with the murders. And no matter how hard Dale pondered on the accusation of Jeff being involved the doubt was still present.

Dale had only known Jeff for the past three years but did, however, come to know him all too well. Jeff was an honest man. Also, Jeff was always focused on solving a crime. Jeff loved his job and Dale knew better than to believe Jeff could transform himself into a replicated monster.

But, then, Dale started to recall Jeff's fascination with Jack Rebus. Nonsense! Jeff was not a homicidal maniac. Dale couldn't be convinced otherwise.

As Dale pulled into Jeff's driveway he saw a shadowy figure moving around on the veranda. Dale entered the veranda and saw Jeff.

Jeff wasn't a bit shocked to look up and see Dale standing there.

"Jeff, I have some things to discuss with you concerning the case," Dale said easily.

"Is it about Linda? The vase? Did the prints come back? What d'ya got for me?" Jeff seemed anxious for Linda's sake.

"Prints came back but not for the vase." Dale was careful in how he attacked the situation. He couldn't just come right out and accuse his best friend of murder. He had to be creative in his approach.

Still, Jeff was anxious. "And whose prints are they? Come on. Are we gonna catch this guy or what? We have to have something now that my sloppy work's not been involved."

That opened Dale's eyes. Jeff just expressed to "not interfering" this time. Was he covering his own tracks? "So you've not been involved? Even investigating without others knowing?" Dale asked expecting to hear Jeff break down and confess to investigating albeit taken off the case. But he didn't.

"No, man. You know better than that. If not in Rappaport I've been at your place or here." Jeff noticed the expression on Dale's face. "Where you gettin' at?"

"I'm just gonna come out and say it. Jeff, your prints are all over everything. Tell me something. Anything. The Chief is pissed. He wants your ass on a platter right now. I gotta bring him something."

Jeff looked uncertain and perplexed. "There's just a big misunderstanding."

About that time four squad cars pulled into the driveway. Three police officers exited their vehicles and got into position to shoot. Chief Wilkins exited his car and walked up to Jeff while reading him the Miranda rights.

Dale yelled out, "You gave me twenty-four hours."

The Chief replied, "That's before the other prints came back."

Jeff asked while being cuffed, "What prints?"

The Chief answered, "On the vase."

Jeff grew infuriated with rage. "You mean to tell me you're accusing me of threatening my own wife. This is fucking bullshit."

No reply from Chief Wilkins was given as Jeff was forced into the back seat of a squad car.

Chapter Thirty

"How is it that I can be the perpetrator of a crime that I, myself, am investigating, Dale? It doesn't make any sense." Jeff sat in the interrogation room.

"I dunno. I don't believe any of this either."

"Did they send you in here to interrogate?"

"No. I think McDermott's been reassigned. Now they're afraid I'll be prejudiced. I'm off the case too."

Suddenly, McDermott entered. He had a shit-eating grin on his face.

Dale slid past him as they shared taunting stares.

The door slammed shut.

"You know why you're here?" asked McDermott.

"Sorta," replied Jeff.

"Sorta? Jeff, you've been arrested for three counts of homicide. Now...did you do it?"

"No! Hell no!"

About that time Chief Wilkins poked his head through the door and said, "McDermott, can we speak?"

McDermott exited the room with a backward strut so he could gleam at Jeff. Jeff returned an uneven smirk.

"What is it, Chief?"

"We gotta let him go. Apparently, prints aren't enough. We need harder evidence." Chief Wilkins thought hard to dismiss the accusations, as well. However, in his years of being on the job he learned one thing: *like whomever you chose but don't trust anybody.*

"But, Chief, what if he kills again?"

"We'll place him under twenty-four-seven surveillance. For now, that's all we can do."

Meanwhile, at the Rappaport Medical Center, Linda's doctor was reviewing her file and going over her blood work when an intrigued expression stretched across his face. A glare of study and focus turned into a vacant expression.

He called out to Kim, the RN. She responded forthwith. She too examined the blood work results. She reacted similarly. Her big question was: "Why wasn't this noticed sooner?"

The doctor replied, "I don't know. It's there in black and white. How could it be missed?"

Later that night, back in Dover, Dale sat in his front room on the couch. He appeared exhausted but refused to sleep. All the concern of Jeff being placed as prime suspect stressed him out.

He decided he needed some fresh air.

He stepped out onto his front porch and his eyes wandered. They were heavy but alert. Within a minute Dale became fixated on a puddle of oil he had spilled a few days earlier. He thought aloud, "When's that going to dry?" But, then, he noticed something else. Aside from the puddle was a footprint. Now Dale thought, "Whose is that?"

The more Dale studied the footprint he noticed a familiarity. Immediately he went inside and grabbed his digital camera. He went back to his porch and quickly scanned through the pictures he had taken while investigating the third murder. He stopped at one. It was of a set of footprints in the victim's garden. He held the camera, with its small glowing screen, next to the oil-based footprint. It was a perfect match.

Now Dale thought hard trying to figure out who it could belong to. He was certain it wasn't his. He elaborated that it to be a possible coincidence. After all, it was a common shoe size and the treading on the sole looked like it could've come from a popular shoe. But Dale insisted on using his detective instincts.

Suddenly, it hit him. The whole ordeal reminded him of another prominence that led him to wonder. On the morning of the last murder, Dale went to Jeff's to see why he left that night. He recalled seeing something strange. Jeff's shoes were caked with mud. Dale never really questioned why—at least in a sense of strangeness.

Dale had to come up with a plan. He needed to get into Jeff's house and find his shoes. The problem being, Jeff's residence was under heavy surveillance.

Dale wanted to prove Jeff innocent. Conversely, none of the evidence was in Jeff's favor.

Dale figured the only way into Jeff's house was to use his power of the badge. He felt that he had every right to enter for the purposes of gathering more evidence if anything.

Dale pulled into Jeff's driveway. Luckily for Dale surveillance officers were few. Also, Dale was somewhat friends with two of them.

They allowed him to enter.

Dale looked around for the mud-caked shoes Jeff wore that night. He wanted to compare the marking on the sole to the footprints he found at his house and the scene of the third murder.

Dale had no luck finding the shoes. In fact, he couldn't find Jeff either. However, he did make one discovery that enforced his superfluous theory. Just outside his back door was a trail of footprints looming to his shed. That's where Jeff kept his motorcycle—his pride and joy.

Dale compared digital images to footprints. Once more they were a perfect match.

Then, Dale walked to Jeff's shed. Jeff was not in there and neither was his motorcycle.

Dale only knew of one place Jeff could be going to… Rappaport Medical Center. But Dale wanted to be discreet. So far everything was still hazy—a mess of correlated assumptions and much needed accusations. Plus if Jeff was behind all of this and headed to the hospital to harm Linda Dale wanted in on all the action.

Chapter Thirty-one

Linda lay serenely with a shadow cast upon her white sheets. It was Jeff. He stood over her breathing heavily. Amanda lay at her bedside. She was unconscious.

Jeff looked like he was bedeviled.

As he inhaled his chest expanded.

What were his intentions?

He reached into his pocket and pulled out a twelve-inch rope. Still…he stood over her. Skulking her like a wolf does its prey.

Suddenly, the doctor came in. "Mr. Roberts? Are you okay?" he asked.

Jeff turned and snarled at the doctor. Frightened by Jeff's appearance and demeanor the doctor yelled, "Get away from her she's preg—" About that time Jeff lashed at him.

Jeff wrestled the doctor to the ground. He was an old man, however, resilient. But Jeff's belligerence and strength were too much for him to handle.

Jeff had the doctor pinned to the ground when, suddenly, someone else entered the room. It was Dale. He ran in just in time to save the doctor's life.

The doctor knew everything about Linda's condition and was her only chance of survival.

With brooding strength, Dale restrained Jeff and told the doctor to contact law enforcement.

Jeff's ruse was confined by Dale's adrenalized vigor.

Jeff was strong by nature but the fact that his ego had flourished into a ravaging sociopath made him that much stronger.

Dale later described apprehending Jeff as being the hardest thing he ever had to do—both mentally and physically.

Dale couldn't accept the fact that his best friend, his mentor, and the only person he could ever trust and confide in was a lunatic. Some said that it was the straw that broke the camel's back.

Soon after the incident, Dale quit the force.

Albeit he was honored and rewarded with medals and praise Dale was emotionally inflicted and reached a point of poor self-worth.

Dale loved Jeff like a brother. And he knew that what Jeff was doing was wrong, however, felt as if he had turned his back on someone that needed guidance rather than incarceration. Maybe he was prejudiced. If the same situation involved an unknown suspect he'd felt differently. He just went on blaming himself.

Jeff's trial was a speedy trial. His verdict was adjudicated acutely and quickly rather than strung out like something high profile.

You must consider: Dover, being the small town that it is, surpassed judgment and sentencing without the process of more profound court systems. Therefore, the only thing the judge needed to rule his verdict was to hold a meeting with the investigators involved and an explanation of the evidence used to incriminate the accused.

Jeff was sentenced to life without the possibility of parole.

Dale drove by Jeff's house. He stopped in the middle of the road. He stared at it for well over a minute when he was startled by a loud and obnoxious car horn. He looked in his rearview mirror and noticed another car behind him. He released the brake and gently eased down on the accelerator.

Chapter Thirty-two

It was midnight as the crescent moon radiated luminescence through Dale's window.

Dale slept soundly on his couch. Not a sound in the world could pull him from his sleep. However, a revenge-seeking Jeff could. Jeff reached downward and grabbed Dale up and slung him to the floor. Dale awoke, still on his couch, relieved to discover it was a horrible nightmare.

It's been well over a week since Jeff was apprehended and sentenced. He was sent to Madison Grove penitentiary. While his motive was still uncertain one thing was: a highfalutin psychiatrist from up north caught wind of the incident and pried his way into the backwash. He arrived at Dover two days after Jeff was sentenced and incarcerated.

The psychiatrist, Dr. Landau by name, immediately became interested in Jeff's mental state. So far he concluded that Jeff was possessed by a higher power. But that sounded redundant in his reports.

Dr. Landau's final conclusion was that Jeff suffered from a split personality.

On a mini MP3 recorder, Dr. Landau documented his thoughts: "The subject seems to enter a void, a dark place if you will. There, he is superior. Most people develop split personalities due to abuse as a child. The subject seems to have developed his over a fascination with a serial killer, however, set off by stress. Perhaps his failure to become a novelist played a part."

Due to Dr. Landau's determination and adept sense of knowledge of the psyche, he was able to get Jeff transferred to an infirmary. The irony here is: three years after Jack Rebus's execution the Buxton House of Corrections shut down. However, it was restored to its original state of function—an infirmary.

During the transfer, something went horribly wrong.

Jeff escaped…with a score to settle.

Once more it was midnight and, yet again, the crescent moon cast fluorescence through Dale's window. Dale, in a deep sleep, lay sprawled out on his couch.

A shadowy figure crept behind the couch. It stopped. It lurked around the couch. It stopped. The ominous movement was a manifestation of repulsion.

Dale was being preyed upon.

It was a tenth of a second—the distance between Dale's eyes appearing and the predator's attack.

Dale was pulled from the couch and slammed to the floor. He didn't know what hit him. However, the attacker revealed himself. It was Jeff Roberts.

Dale fought his way through every inch of the house trying to escape. Jeff toyed with him. He allowed Dale to move freely but refused to let him break away from his contrivance of torture. And Dale knew he was circumvented.

Dale refused to surrender. He determined that he was had either way. This, however, gave him the ability to worry less about death and more about survival. Dale had survival instincts. Even if it meant death he wouldn't go alone.

Dale looked high and low for a weapon.

He needed something.

He saw his Glock on a table nearby and flinched to retrieve it, however, thought about his little brother and was reminded of his phobia.

Do you believe that one fear can cancel another fear? In this case, it's true.

With all Dale could muster defying laws of absolute strength he lunged for the gun. He landed hard on the floor. The landing nearly knocked the breath out of him. Yet he managed to maintain a firm grip.

Jeff lunged too but it wasn't for the gun. Jeff was headed straight for Dale. But something happened between the distances. A loud blast was released as Jeff was lifted from the floor and dissipated, full throttle, in reverse.

Blood was everywhere.

Dale, using the wall behind him for support, eased his way up and carefully walked over to Jeff. He stood over and examined the body. He wanted to be certain that Jeff was down for good. And between Jeff's, still gleaming, eyes was a bullet hole.

Chapter Thirty-three

"For all who are led by the Spirit of God are sons of God. For you did not receive the spirit of slavery to fall back into fear, but you have received the spirit of son-ship. When we cry, 'Abba! Father!' it is the Spirit himself bearing witness with our spirit that we are children of God, and if children, then heirs, heirs of God and fellow heirs with Christ, provided we suffer with him in order that we may also be glorified with him. I consider that the sufferings of this present time are not worth comparing with the glory that is to be revealed to us. For the creation waits with eager longing for the revealing of the sons of God; for the creation was subjected to futility, not of its own will but by the will of him who subjected it in hope; because the creation itself will be set free from its bondage to decay and obtain the glorious liberty of the children of God. We know that the whole creation has been groaning in travail together until now; and not only the creation, but we ourselves, who have the first fruits of the Spirit, groan inwardly as we wait for adoption as sons, the redemption of our bodies. Ashes to ashes, dust to dust...."

We live our life beneath the hand of God—bound by his glory. As we grow from toddler to adulthood we are given a path. Spiritually we jaunt amongst the everlasting way. But sooner or later we come to a fork. One way can lead you to darkness to whereas the other can lead you to the light of heaven. We are required to decide on what path to follow. You can only choose left or right. Jeff must have kept on walking…straight down the middle.

The light of heaven did shine down that day. Its radiance reflected off of Jeff's enameled casket creating a blinding mass.

Many attended, except for Linda. Perhaps she saw him walking toward the light. Linda, not dead but in between the layers of life and death, could've had a spiritual encounter.

Something must've happened for as the sun shined down on Jeff it shined through the window and caressed Linda, as well. She smiled. But this time the doctor walked in just in time to witness it.

He screamed out, "She's at stage two! Stage two!"

Nonetheless, flowers bloomed and radiance charged the small town of Dover. In short…all was restored.

And as the ceremony proceeded warmth fell amongst those in attendance.

Rather than condemn the man for his evil doings they honored the man that once protected the township from evil doings.

They considered him a victim of circumstance.

Dale knew Jeff all too well. Albeit Dale was responsible for Jeff's death he knew Jeff wanted to kill the monster too. That was Jeff's default nature.

We inhabit lives of uncertainty and strive to find answers. In a sense, we're all victims of circumstance. The only difference is Jeff swore to an oath. He swore to abide by and comply with the law.

Jeff was an enforcer. And as Dale saw it he would do everything in his power to have his best friend and long time partner remembered that way.

It was not in Jeff's cards to be remembered as a killer. However, Circumstance had a better hand causing him to fold.

Dale, in contrast, felt abandoned and alone. Also, he worried for Linda. If and when she was to ever come out of her coma she would go insane knowing that her husband was deceased.

How would Dale explain this to her?

Jeff was indeed a sick man. He had a part of him that overshadowed his true physical form and mental state. Ironically Jeff was investigating a trio of homicides that he, himself, executed.

Between the soul's eye and the mind's eye, there exists a center point. It is divided into two sections: *good and evil*. The only way to determine each element and classify its distinction is to cross a line. However, once crossed the mind and soul connect causing confinement to the element chosen. These elements are the lines of distinction.

The Darkness

It was dark—pitch-black—the kind of darkness that can dampen a flame into a clump of charred ashen clay. I had just snuffed out the last candle on the mantle as smoke scattered, fading into the darkness. The fire in the hearth still blazed, but not for long. It too went out…by itself. It may have been a gust of wind from the cracked window. Perhaps, it may have been dampness seething from the cellar just below from the tiny cracks in the hardwood. One thing was for certain:—it was ominous, nonetheless.

I tossed. I turned. I couldn't sleep. Nightmares and visions of the horrible tragedy haunted my dreams like a vengeful spirit after my very soul kept me awake and restless. Razor sharp claws of black, luminous, translucent fabric lashed at me as I lay motionless, hardly undetected. It was him; *the one who came before*. I didn't know what that meant at that time but it stuck in my head as if to have some significant meaning. I was too paralyzed with fear to care—praying for my marred existence.

At this point, I questioned my state of being. Was I awake or was it all just a dream? It was too real—lost inside a demented headspace like an A.R.G. Maybe I was asleep. Whatever the case, It was still a nightmare. If I was awake I was as good as dead. The look of sheer terror on my face would haunt the coroner forever. And if I was asleep, I would be haunted forever. Suddenly, I heard a voice. And so I replied:

"Jaime?"

"Hello? Who are you?" I looked around confusedly. "What are you?"

"I am 'The One'…"

"Who came before?" I asked caustically.

"Yes."

It sounds silly, I know. But that was the gist of the conversation. Brief. I remembered earlier so it came as no surprise.

Then I started to hear whispers. Somewhere within the verbal gale, I heard my name repeatedly. Then I started to feel the sensation of someone holding my hand. It was so surreal—almost like a dream, but I wasn't asleep. This time I was certain. I was very alert and oriented. Maybe it was more like a bad acid trip—lucid but surreal. Nonetheless, in the end, it doesn't really matter. We're all a little mad.

A few hours had lapsed since my last episode. I awoke feeling dizzy—disoriented.

I stumbled into the kitchen and flipped on the light. I entered the pantry. Coffee. That's the cure. So I grabbed the darkest roast and set up the pot. Beads of sweat, forming on my forehead, dribbled upon my brow. Quickly it soaked in and continued to dribble into my eyes. I closed them and swiped my lids free of sweat. Suddenly, my heart began to palpitate as my heart rate breached regularity. It all began again.

At first, the lights began to flicker rhythmically. And just as soon as I closed my eyes the darkness ensued its evil presence upon me again—gnashing at me—latching onto my soul like a demonic parasite. I was befuddled beyond the highest caliber. I wouldn't survive the night. The damn thing weighed me down like a dominant force. Again, I felt the sensation of another's hand caressing mine—gently squeezing. It was warm and friendly. They meant me no harm. Whoever this person was trying to break through to me had some personal connection with my circumstances—a harbinger, if you will.

A few hours had lapsed since my last episode. I awoke feeling dizzy—disoriented.

The lights were bright, but as I looked around the lights shone brighter. I was restricted of movement—confined to rails. The bed I was in was not my California King. I was somewhat relieved to see tubes of medicine looming from my arm. Even more relieved to see I was surrounded by family and friends, as well as my wife of five years, Abigail, holding my hand. It was then the doctor approached me. He explained to me that I'd been in a coma for a week. I couldn't believe it.

Not long after, cops poured in by the dozen; or so it seemed. I learned the reason for my state of being, nonetheless. I was shot near death while trying to make coffee in my kitchen. I later learned that they apprehended my hired gun. At the time, he was known only as: "The One Who Came Before." What had I experienced during seven days of slumber?

Mr. Anderson's Shadow

It is believed by the natives of Favre Island that if you had done somebody wrong at one point in your life their ghost will take shape of a menacing shadow and haunt you to your grave. The following story you are about to read is based on a true account and a recorded conversation. Although legal rights prohibit me to pen this document in verbatim, the dialogue is very similar to the actual recording.

The setting is Wingate Mansion on Favre Island. The cast is Doc Smith and Master William Wingate. The story revolves around, the deceased, Mr. Anderson. And so we begin.

Doc Smith leaned up against a cold, gray, stone-textured wall and lit a cigarette. He took a deep drag and began to assist the anti-distraught Master William Wingate with resolving an issue concerning the passing of his dear friend Mr. Anderson and the possibility of the deceased's ghost lingering within the walls of the mansion. "Master William, if you only knew how preposterous this sounds. A ghost? Here? At Wingate Mansion? It's completely absurd." Doc Smith had a history of overreacting to the smallest things.

Suddenly, a mild, strong draft gusted through the room scattering papers and gathering attention from both parties. Doc Smith raised an eyebrow as Master William replied with an argument. "I know. I know. But I tell you, I know what I saw. Doc, it was as plain as you're standing here now." It was obvious Master William wasn't a bit concerned about the surprising incident. And, apparently, neither was Doc Smith. Yet, he grabbed hold of a nearby pillar in an attempt to sustain his balance.

Doc Smith cleared his throat as he loosened his collar, "Ahem…" Then he rubbed the back of his neck as though he felt a tingle. "Have you ever had an eye exam? I know an exceptional ophthalmologist just outside of—"

"Ophthalmologist? Really?" Meanwhile, a softer draft trailed behind the previous gust, which caused Doc Smith's lapel to move, but only slightly. "My vision is 20/10, Doc. Why, I can see for miles with perfect clarity. My eyesight being good or bad isn't the case. I was right there, not even ten feet away. Spend the night! I will show you! I will prove to you that I'm not a loon!"

Doc Smith shivered as a small chill infiltrated his body. Still, he remained unconvinced. "Master William, I simply suggested an eye exam. I mentioned nothing about your mental state. You're taking this whole thing way too far…blowing speculation out of proportion. And as for me spending the night, I'm working the ER. Believe you/me, under different circumstances I would take you up on a sleepover." Doc Smith tilted his head for a moment in remembrance. "I haven't done such a thing since my youth.

"Tell me, Master William, did you by any chance have a nightcap? You know, the meds you are on will counteract the alcohol causing hallucinations and delusions."

The argument escalated and took a slight turn, but not for the better. The outside winds made the exterior doors shutter as a branch crashed through a bay window. Still, the two men seemed unconcerned. "I don't believe I'm hearing you correctly. I haven't dropped a drink since the night Veronica left."

"Really?—'cause you sound a little *inebriated* right now."

"I'm ashamed of you, Doctor. Is that the best you can do? Deter the situation at hand using my prior bouts with the bottle as a crutch. Why, you're the great Doc Smith. You can give a better analysis than alcoholism."—*(in a single breath)*—"Or has your remedial clairvoyance, your ability to sense any condition before it manifests into something worse without assistance from *Webmd*, abandoned you?"

That infuriated Doc Smith. "Don't you turn this on me, William! I'm only trying to be rational. I mean, ghosts just don't exist. Debunking the occurrence with my medical tactic is all I know to do. Remember...you called me, dear friend. I'm doing you the favor."

Master William shook his head in disappointment. "Clever, Doctor. How so very clever. I call to you in good faith, you come over and suggest that I'm crazy, and then you consider your cynicism a favor. Good faith, Doctor. This isn't your clinic. Therefore, I'm not your patient right now. I called my friend. A friend that just so happens to be a doctor. Why, right now, I wouldn't even claim you as *my friend*."

Doc Smith was much too stubborn to give up that easily. Therefore, he switched gears and made one last attempt at rationality. "If that's the way you feel right now then why do you keep referring to me as *Doctor*? Rather than further this discussion why don't you use your authority and tell me to get out? Something is keeping me here." Now the tables were turned. And Master William showed a slight affliction to Doc Smith's retort.

"The hope that you will, *at least*, try to understand me rather than scorn me."

"On that note, I will take leave. I just can't bring myself to participate in such foolishness. I refuse to put my license on the line." There was no use. Master William was even more stubborn than Doc Smith; therefore, convincing him, otherwise, was like beating a dead horse.

"How would you possibly lose your doctrine, Doctor? A diminished reputation?"

"Bye, William. I wish you well. I hope this little snag in our friendship doesn't provoke you to look for another doctor. Your well being is, *and always will be*, my concern." Doc Smith held up his right fist and pointed at Master William. "Doctor's code of ethics. Farewell, *my friend*."

As Doc Smith took his exit he was approached by a shadowy figure in the foyer with a partition obstructing Master William's view. Softly spoken, he gave instruction. "Continue with the treatment until further notice. The subject hasn't a clue, thus far." Then Doc Smith nonchalantly exited the mansion and boarded his pontoon boat. Into the dark void of night, he faded till he was seen no more.

The storm settled as a violent scream came from within the mansion walls and pierced through the ominous night. The moon reflected on the waters as they rippled and shimmered—a ghostly hue.

Narrative of Otis Platt

Preface

Written by J.L. Bosworth, Esq., III
December 11, 1975
5:00 a.m., Central Time

...in a kingdom far, far away...hogwash...you can't start a story that way. Therefore, I will begin anew.

Allow me to introduce you to an old friend of mine. His name was Otis Platt. We served in Vietnam together; and ever since he hasn't been the same. You see he was shell-shocked. That, itself, took a toll on him. However, it didn't stop there. He was placed in pain management therapy and throughout his course, he became addicted to a very harsh drug known today as morphine.

Otis has always been a very smart fella. Smart! Oh, yes, my friends...very smart indeed. Throughout school, he maintained his high honor roll averages. And even after school, he continued to collect high honors from many different states and statures. He was so smart, however, that he figured out a way to think himself to death. That's right; I am writing this in mourning due to my friend's passing. He died just yesterday in the very same padded cell I am confined to now. Or so I've been told. He was sick for some time.

Before his death, he spoke to me of his many misadventures. His timeline didn't make any sense, nonetheless, ensuring that it was just one of his many delusions. He would visit me often during my confinement and take leave without a see-you-later or goodbye. Listen to me now—I am the one who isn't making sense. Perhaps it's the adverse reactions to my many medications I am given. Antipsychotics do tend to mess with the brain's chemistry. And I am on many.

If and when I ever decide to break free, I wish to visit his grave. Albeit my memory of him is faint, I am still aware of his past existence. Nowadays, I remember very little. Again, I'm certain it's the meds. I do recall one occurrence, however—the day we met. It was exactly five years ago today. I will take you back.

The date was December 11, 1970. I was sitting at my writing desk working on my next installment of the Dark Angel series. Suddenly, I heard a knock on my door. Actually, the visitor knocked thrice and very loudly, at that. I flinched from unawareness and went to answer the door. There stood a man—approximately my weight, height, and age. He introduced himself as Otis Platt: an admirer of my work. It was then I did something I thought I never would have done before; I invited him in.

We sat and discussed writing over Earl Gray. Instantly, he struck me as an intelligent man. However, there was something off about him. He acted as if he had known me his whole life. Nevertheless, he did quickly grow on me. He was the kinda person one thinks they already know. He didn't act as though my other admirers do. He never even asked for my autograph. He strode to impress the normal side of me rather than the artist. It wasn't long after that I befriended him.

He named off a few of my titles, including some of my earlier work that didn't market too well—rarities. I was impressed by this and began to feel more comfortable around him. However, one strange thing occurred. Soon after we met I began to have blackouts. They got worse as time went on and I started seeing less of him, and eventually, he mysteriously disappeared. If memory serves me correctly my last encounter with him was only a month after we met. And for this, I had just recently learned of his death. In his absence, I worried sick about him. I was devastated when I learned of his passing. But within the month that contained him, we had quite the 'fair. Good times. Be it as it may, I am distraught to learn of his death, but also pleased to know he is gone. You see, toward the end, he began to take over my life. I was relieved to know that our "convene" came to a screeching halt. Never once did he encumber me, though. I was incarcerated towards the end of that same month and year. Perhaps that is what came of him. I am not well and I am sure that is off-putting. A whackjob is what they call me.

The following content of this manuscript is recorded documentation of his so-called misadventures. Take note: none of the details are fabricated by any means, whatsoever. But also, remember: I only write what information is given to me. Albeit I write fiction, I'm a journalist by heart and fruitful nature.

Furthermore, I made Otis a promise just before he stopped coming around. He told me in confidence that he had been suffering from a state of depression…that he had his first noticeable bout since the day we met. I told him that I would keep it a secret and that I wouldn't hold it against him. That is what led me to believe, for the longest time, that suicide had something to do with his disappearance. I wasn't a bit surprised when I learned recently that he was found dead. However, I have yet to learn where he is buried. Every time I mention his death people seem to ignore me like it's some sort of covert operation.

I'm turning in now. I will write more tomorrow. Until then, goodnight and sweet dreams.

I: the arrival

It felt as though I've been here before. The quadrants of this specific cinerarium of sight and sound. But that was nonsense. Absolute nonsense. The trees, the earth, and even the air seemed somewhat familiar. I have taken so much for granted and now, life was on the list—the list I took for granted. What led me here? What magnificent force—I refer to it as that but am still uncertain of the exact values.

Time is a very fragile thing. I should know…I was a clocksmith for many years. I knew not to toy with it. At that, I would even warn others. You break it, you buy it, I'd say. Now that I mention it, perhaps that's what damaged my business. I was on the verge of closing, after all. That is when I was reminded of the timepiece I had dusted off and pocketed just before I awoke here. Convincing myself it was naught less a dream, and nothing more.

At that very moment, I urged myself to do myself a favor. Sounds rather odd, doesn't it? No need for questioning, I'm more than certain it was. Why, confidence was my most valued virtue. No, it wasn't arrogance, I had told the voice inside my head. But the voice replied back. It was definitely not alone. It made me aware that it was setting up a minute township just off the left peninsula of my gray matter. I have a chronic cough, which I must include. The likes of tourists trampling on my medulla.

My opiate receptors barked and howled like vicious demonic creatures. They awaited my next drop of morphine. And if I didn't appease them, they made me pay. And they hurt me badly. So bad that I felt as if I was dying from a rare form of the flu. I do believe they refer to this ailment now as Ebola. They were barking ever so ferociously. This is the southwest. There has to be a poppy field growing nearby, I rationalized adding, why if I did so run up on one I would select the most swollen bulb and feast upon its sap like the juice of a deliciously, sweet fruit...savoring its bitter, narcotic milk like a baby at a tit.

Yummy.

However, I was taken aback. Back to the entrails of my being here. It was a dream and I was the pursuer, I convinced myself. Then be it! I shall take the tour. Perhaps, I will come across a crop of heavenly poppy fruit, as I often referred to it.

Euphoria to me was close to experiencing a rebirth. Some stronger than the others. Some medications being synthetic and less potent. However, it was opium mixed with vodka I chose overall. The old timers refer to this as Laudanum. Listen to me rant, would you? Would you just listen? I was, after all, a servant of the 1800s. Late, late 1800s. Even better, 1896, to be exact.

Automobiles appeared different. A larger variety, of course. Buildings, buildings galore. But where is the clock shop? Where I stood still now would have to be its previous location, but the closest building insight was a Hand-e-Mart. Mmm, spelled incorrectly, nonetheless. That doesn't speak highly of the bafoons I had yet to encounter. So be it—I was on my merry way to learn more about this sacred villa. A town, it was called. I'm certain it still is, somewhere in time.

Along my travels, I was a trite bit worried that things would be indifferent upon my return. Then it dawned on me—just as the splatter of mud that encased my leisure wear. My god, I paid a hard-earned fifteen dollars for this attire, and now just ruined. Ruined, I say. Anyway, where I last stood had to be a portal. Not far from the previous location; I went back and took off my jacket. It was ruined now and besides, rather hot. Did I mention it was ruined!?! I tied it taut around a pole. Or was it a giant candy cane? Goodness no, that would mean I'd be in some fairy tale world filled with chocolate streams and cookie houses. But curiosity had its way with me as it always did. I looked, of course, assuming there was no one else around. And then…it tasted rather odd.

Right off the bat, I noticed their ways, their nuance of culture and attire. To them, I looked rather odd. That is when I decided to visit the closest pants and shirt store I came across.

I entered one, however, was scoffed at when I discovered it was for lady apparel. I should have known by the many displays in the window. The white Victorian gown and veil gave it away. Now I know this. Why didn't it just say for ladies on the sign? That is when I felt embarrassed for I embarked upon the sign. Wouldn't you know it? The damn store was called Ladies Night. A rather odd name for a merchant's business. But then again, my store went only by my family name. PLATT—TIME IS WHERE IT'S AT!!! I laughed. I inherited the business from my father, and he from his father, and…well, you get the picture. What started as a roadside market serving travelers on horse's work-wear, had turned into what I know it as now. Added on for each century it was erected, the platform I worked at was that of a castle.

Small children were frightened by this. It didn't matter; there was only a market for adult textiles whilst children wore rags patched together with ancestral cloth.

Before I knew it, I stood before, what I was more than certain, was a Man's store. The last store being Called Ladies Night and this one was called MEN'S Night. What I walked into, however, I was completely thrown by its nature. A brothel. Dear god…you honestly had to work your way through an orgy labyrinth to precede its business. I have never seen breasts so large and well formed like works of sculpturing clay. And the men, I estimated one to be well over ten inches in length and eight inches in girth. I was only five at the last measure. I was a teen, however. I lifted my pants and peeked. Yep, still five. I was hard from the excitement. A nude woman stood before me and slid down my pants. The orgy went into hysterics. I pulled up my pants and left that coven of vampires.

I was indeed lost. Too far away from my starting point. I didn't fret. However…once more, I *slapwitted* myself for neglecting to leave a trail. I smoothed out the edges with the optimism that it would have only been swept away from the towns-keep.

Then it hit me like an anvil from the clear blue sky. Men's Wear | rugged work wear | jeans, t-shirts, uniforms, etc. I went there.

I entered and immediately smelled an unfamiliar smell. Perhaps it was the newness of things. I was quite shocked at the prices. A plaid shirt costing fifty dollars. A pair of denim pants, thirty. Why, I didn't have that kinda loot. Therefore, hindsight's twenty/twenty (so they say), I immediately sought out the owner. (I was good at the immediate things, in case you're wondering.) He was the huge gentleman behind the service desk. I approached him carefully. The old man displayed a *trapshooter* on the wall and I found it quite intimidating. I said, Sir? By means of grabbing his attention. Perhaps, however, I didn't speak loud enough so I repeated—Sir?

I hear you, he replied, I'm ain't def.

Ain't?—I thought. Good heavens, what does he mean?

He turned and laughed at my roughshod exterior, for I donned the most primitive wear of anyone there known. There not known, as well, I'm certain.

I'm rather outdated, sir. I have no money for these bargains. Perhaps you would be interested in a trade?

He squinted his brow and asked, trade? What? What do you have that I want?

An outfit for an outfit.

Not quite. He reached behind his desk and laid flat a blank sheet of paper. Here, sign this.

But it's blank, I thought.

Just to let me know we have an agreement. There's writing, it's just unnoticeable to the naked eye.

If you say, I said as I scribed my name. Then, before my very eyes, words appeared. I was at six and sevens by this anomaly. I made a failed attempt to read it, but he pulled it from my sight. Yanked it, rather rudely, was more a suitable term.

He told me, take whatever you wish. One outfit per customer though.

Let's see…one outfit. I chose the plaid shirt and denim jeans I first laid my eyes upon. Where do I try it on, kind sir?

No need. One size fits all. Now be gone with ya.

He shooed me away. In all my years of being a man, I had never been shooed. This was unlike any established community I have never known. He honestly shooed me. That man.

I left. Well, wouldn't you? I would have soon enough. I was eager to learn more about this so-called town. I had yet to discover more. That is when, a few blocks straightforward, I approached a small building. *HeadShop*, I read. I also read the contents displayed and opium was on the list. I thought nothing of it. I had yet to discover that in present times it was an illegal substance. I mean, it grows a beautiful flower, nonetheless. I was so naïve there. So very naïve that I entered with a smile and headed straight for the front desk. Before I could spit it out the man had already set it on the counter. Ten dollars? I had that. I wrestled my pockets for money when it was made clear that I had left them in my former pants. And to make matters worse, so did I the watch. I *slapwitted* myself once more arguing with the voice inside my head. The man looked at me strongly and laid another blank sheet of paper on his counter. I would outsmart him. That's right. I weighed my left hand upon it as I signed with my right. I then began to read. The…the paper vanished before my very eyes. What was going on? What dimension or planet did I aboard? Invisible ink, disappearing paper, 'tis the doings of black magic—a deadman's keep, I quaffed the words down my throat embedded with saliva.

About now, I was very intrigued by my discoveries, and more discoveries that awaited me. I only wish I had not lost my watch. I was lost in time, literally, and the watch was my ticket home. That is when I backtracked. I headed straight for the men's clothing store. The owner was gone. Perhaps a lunch break, I thought. I waited what seemed like hours and still, he was not there. I began to mettle my way through the clothes. It wasn't long before I discovered my old digs. I searched the pocket. I found the money. However, it would do me no good here. But I had no luck obtaining the watch.

I would venture further back. But that would mean I'd have to face my humiliation once more at the brothel house. I made a quick decision to bypass that and head straight for the Ladies' store. I hoped and prayed I'd find my watch there.

During my search, I noticed something odd. Rather odd, indeed. I could find my way to each store I had visited but still, I had no clue how to get back to point A. It must have to do with the watch. I find my watch, I find my way. It didn't matter either way. For every stone turned I found nothing beneath. Well, it must be closing hours and I haven't time to wait and see. There was no one there either. I left in search of my way back to the *HeadShop* where I last was. During this time I had become lost once again. You fool, sounded the voice inside my head. I then sat beneath a tree, a naked tree at that, I sorted my thoughts. Suddenly I heard soft rattling percussion at my side. I turned for fear of the worst and was exacerbated to discover a two-headed snake calmly beside me. I spoke to the snake and it spoke back. Rather odd, but I didn't seem surprised. I wasn't quite sure where I was, but it was made very clear where I wasn't—home.

Billy Van

II: the model

I hadn't the slightest idea. Space and time no longer existed. People, once was, were people no more. And it was all because of an irresponsible folly on my behalf. I didn't stop. No. I kept on keeping on. I brought the snake with me for protection. Not that I needed any, I hoped. From who? From what? I was beyond the outer limits of confusion at this point and didn't know my way back. Just where was this so-called *sopwith* road leading me? Why was I here? And most importantly, where the dickens was my watch? The watch contained all the answers. Yes, indeed it did. I was certain of that. I look back at the inscription, very small, hard to read, and recall just what it said: Time carries all. Do you carry time? Fair enough. I didn't. Okay, I admit it...I didn't. Oh, I already said that.

I thought long and hard. If I was a watch where would I be?

Up ahead, I noticed a sculpture—a model of fine art. Dionysus holding grapes and the grapevine turning into a two-headed serpent just as I be-friended. I examined the model, sculpture, statue, whatever it was, studious-ly. It took me aback home reminding me of a (there) current story by the master of weird fiction—the great H.P. Lovecraft. Pickman's Model I doted. The words I choose may not make sense to you, however, do to me. You must remember, I am from a different century and my grammar and even spelling may be defined as poor. I'm recording these thoughts in the index of my mind as they unfold before me. Hindsight's twenty/twenty. Honestly, I never knew what that meant. I just enjoy saying it.

The lines were well curved, the masculinity was well carved and the face was well chiseled. In all my years I have never seen this rendition of the Greek god. It was almost as if it was telling me something. The voice in my head began and mid-sentence it transferred to the model. Again, I was not overtaken by excitation. I did, however, make one facet of logic. The voice the snake spoke was not his. How foolish. Snakes cannot speak. At least not in my world. The reason I process such thoughts is the very same reason for my state-of-being. I once carried time, but no more. Thence, time will not carry me.

As I did the snake, I spoke to the model. It was clever, indeed. Must be because it was my inner-voice rattling aloud. I asked him, would you care to go on an excursion with me and Mr. Snake?

Try lifting me, said the model.

I grunted as sweat beads filled my hair and doused my forehead. Impossi-ble, I exclaimed. You must take me as a joke, mind you. Do you agree?

How's about you, Mr. Snake? Of course, the snake could no longer speak. It was converted to dumb. However, it still soothed my protection.

Just over there beyond the moonshine still and barrels is a wagon. It was originally used to transfer me. However, most recently used to transfer the still.

Is moonshine illegal here?—I asked. It was in good ole 1896, however, often overlooked.

Haven't you figured it out by now? Nothing in Athens is illegal.

Athens, is that what this is or are you just referring to it as such because of who you are...ahem...what you are?

Yes, you are in Athens.

The strangest things have happened to me, thus far, model. I was forced to sign two documents that both had reappearing ink, one vanished from mid-sight.

You fool, I was there. Need you forget? I am with you everywhere you go. Even if you were to not take my physical form, my mentality, your mentality will conjoin.

Oh, but I do plan on taking you with me. Just as soon as Mr. Snake and I figure out how we gonna get you on that cart. As long as it rolls well it won't be a hustle at all.

But that's just the thing...it's been sitting there for five centuries.

That was how far I traveled was five centuries.

Then bring me the cart. I have an idea.

I brought him the cart, just as he instructed, and I couldn't believe my eyes what happened next. He jumped on the darn thing. If you can do that then why can't you walk?

I can. It's just too damn far for my aching body.

Before we left he gave me one last instruction. Put the snake at my side and release it. The snake crawled up the grapevine and turned to stone before my very eyes. But again, I was not surprised.

Together we jaunted along our merry way. We talked about many things. One of which was *Boscow stars*. I had not known what *Boscow stars* were so he explained to me by saying that five centuries ago, and twelve centuries before man, an unaccredited god was sentence to life entrapped in the fourth galaxy. His name was...

Ah, Boscow. I get it. Just as the Atlas is the atlas and Narcissus is narcissus and Achilles is achilles.

I'm not sure what you just said but, yeah…something of that nature. The model changed the subject. We should be getting close now. Just over that hill.

Close to what? I was unaware we had a destination.

The house of five-cornered-walls.

What in the hell is that?—I asked confusedly.

It's your next stop. I neglected to tell you that you have to reach five destinations before you can obtain your watch. One for each century. The last object is the portal that will send you home.

I couldn't believe what I was hearing. Home. Finally, home sweet home. A little outdated compared to my current whereabouts, but I will not need to readjust. After all, it is my century…finally, something I am familiar with.

So we continued our travel. Close, my ass. Try a good mile away. Not to mention the hill I will have to pull this thing over. When I grow tired, he will just have to get off and walk the rest of the way. I'm sure he knows. I mean that's his job isn't it—to know what I'm thinking before I—

Yes, Otis. I will get off and walk. You had best pick up your pace before you miss your deadline.

Deadline!—Deadline!—what is this about a deadline!?!

Otis, I'm appalled.

What?

You have so much to learn. So much, in fact, that I can't teach you. That is why you will be enlightened along the way as the voice transfers from source to source.

I was caught unaware of all this *rigamaroo*. But still, the main question stood before me…what brought me here in the first place? I won't lie. At first, I thought that I was in hell:—*rigamaroo*. And then I thought, perhaps I had died and this is limbo:—*rigamaroo*. Thus far, I only had two assumptions for I was gathering them along the way. The model grinned. He knew all my thoughts more than I did. He knew what I was thinking right now, in fact. Good, we're almost to the hill. He said it, I didn't. My voices are now getting mixed up. I don't know who's saying what, at this point. I will tell you one thing—this is me talking—your dear narrator Otis. This is an experience that will last a lifetime. I will definitely take it with me when I go. Go where? Ah, there it goes again. It must be trying to get into my head for the journey is almost at its end.

III: the five-cornered wall

I entered the house with the model at my side. He froze—statuesque as the voice went back into my head. Oh dear god. I hated it there. It gave me such a vessel-throbbing migraine one could not fathom. But it didn't stay for long. I heard it once more, this time outside of me. (I forgot to mention, by the way, that each time the transfer happens I get an overwhelming sense of heightened well-being. And it lasts the whole time through.) I searched for the source putting two and two together. I also spoke to it so that I could track it down easily. Smart, huh? Not really. I often gave myself way too much credit.

Where are you?—I asked tenderly.

Behind you. I turned. Behind you. I turned. Behind you. I turned. Behind you. I turned one last time, I promise. Behind you. It didn't make any sense. Then it grew louder. It resonated within the cracks of all five corners of the wall. The voice was now inside the wall. Clever. However, I could not take the house with me. Or could I? It assured me that it would have to go. Something about two blank pages being signed by me. That's it, I snapped my fingers. That's why I signed the two. But how will you go?

Upon my asking that question, the rooftop jutted out reptilian wings. It dismounted from its mainstay as talons clinched claws embedded deep inside the earth. Wow, my eyes lit up. No, literally. It would need two beams of light to shine the way. This was becoming extremely amazing. Each and every task, down to its sole core, was becoming a new and exciting challenge.

I climbed the trellis up the side of the house and found myself a good place to sit. Near the chimney. There was a slight dip in the roof from the pitch changes in its construction. All the while it would be the perfect place for me to navigate. Not too close to the edge and not too far from the edge. I quaffed a shot of opium *tink* I had stowed away in my pants pocket and sloshed it around in my mouth, gargled it, and swallowed it saying, now I'm ready. I figured the added euphoria would be necessary for this new adventure. Plus, I was an addict and withdrawal's a bitch. It suppressed my cough, took away the pain in my joints from my travels as well as stopped my traveler's diarrhea, and eased my state of mind, doing all the wondrous things the tincture was designed to do. A gift from the heavens, I often said. And I believe that is true. We are surrounded by so much plantlife and foliage that unknown species and their uses, be it medicinal or culinary, has ta do. I believe it to be written in the stars. The four stars of Boscow, I now know, thanks to the model. Before the house took flight, however, it commanded the model to enter. Inside the house was a space reserved for it. Slowly, all this was coming together. The snake, the model, the house. And I was ever so glad to take part.

The house lifted and spread its wings open wide, catching the wind and filtering it as fuel. Wheee!!! I excitedly screamed. My mouth caught air and muted its volume, however.

The house and I spoke using the chimney as feed. What's next, I asked. It's all you, Otis. All you.

What did that even mean?—all me. So I asked, What?

I will tell you as we draw near. This next piece is very far away, deep inside the Himalayas.

The Himalayas?—what? I thought that. However, the house repeated it in the exact same voice as me. It was a part of me, after all—the house, and its contents.

Up until the point where we hit a patch of turbulence, I was doing great. I almost fell, however. The fall would have been quite a distance. But I took another quaff of the magic *tink* and resided. All better now. We swooshed, tipped, spun, and turned. I—(a fully grown man)—was experiencing the joys of my youth. Suddenly, I lost my bearings and fell. I was so worried this would happen. However, the front door flung open and a carpet reached out and snagged me like a tongue. I was now inside the house, where I should have been all the while. And you know what?—the house looked somewhat familiar…empty…clean…but familiar.

I noticed a bare space on the wall that took shape of a picture. A nail and hammer appeared out of nowhere beneath it. A picture, I thought to myself.

Rightamundo, my dear, sweet Otis. Right you are. And I bet it's a self-portrait of me. I thought it but the house spoke it. I now knew what this meant. We must have been drawing near. So close, the sound of mountainous wildlife echoed in the far. I looked out the bay window (the eyes of the house) and saw the white peaks just up ahead—snowcapped mountains. I have always wanted to climb a high knob to the point I could almost touch the sky.

Unexpectedly, a storm attacked:—chilling breath and razor sharp spit. Lightening then thunder, which indicated we were in the eye of the storm. We're almost there, Otis. Closer…much closer. The storm is just an obstacle made for me to surpass. I have done this many times before. There are no cobwebs in my five corners. The wind did, however, press against us slowing our timeframe. Time…what time?—I thought. I haven't got time. It was then I truly understood what that meant. Literally, of course, but true.

Windgullies flew overhead. So close I could reach out and snag one. And just then, we crashed. We didn't crash...a rough landing was all. I rattled my brain to gather my senses and struggled to keep my bearings. This would call for another quaff of *tink*. Careful, said the house. You will overdose, Otis. What you are consuming is pure poison of its highest caliber. You don't want to end up like your father, do you?

What...how did you?—Oh yeah...must I forget. You are my conscience. That's right, Otis. The house spoke back in my turn. This only meant it was getting close to reentering my head, and the migraine...I didn't allow this tedious fray to stand in my way. Oh no. Two more adventures (as I call them) and I would be home. I loved the sound of that. My home sweet home.

The house spoke its last words, you must exit. A mile down the beaten path you will see the next installment.

I did as I was told. Now, this is becoming very confusing. Stay with me. I exited the house and entered a vast jungle. Rain porous leaves, tumultuous maneaters afoot. The kind that men fear. I do...at least I did. After this day, everything changed. And to think, it all started with humiliation at the brothel house. I could not have been any more frightened by the curse of my predecessors. Damn them and their tiny peckers. But these were just reoccurring thoughts that played repeatedly in my head like a min-recorder. They still make those, do they?

I gathered the rest of my thoughts and went on. I had a task to fulfill and time was wearing thin. Again, I was reminded. I had no time. Not without that blasted watch. Damn my irresponsible ways!!! God, if only the house had given me directions. I was definitely lost in the wilderness. Beasts were all around me. I felt them near. And just as I snapped a twig a *wolohan* lunged for me. My dear god, I have never seen one up close. I didn't know whether to shake in my boots, piss down both legs or be gentle to the creature. Without the snake, I could use some protection the rest of my way. However, the *wolohan* had other plans. It skulked over me like it was outlining its attack. Let's see, I could go straight for the jugular and quench my thirst. I could bite down on him and savor the meat as he squirmed to escape. Better yet, I could befriend him and devour him when I felt the hungriest. These were the *wolohan's* thoughts, not mine.

I traversed her kill. I knew I had it in me. And she was all the protection I needed to fulfill my next to last task. She dolefully approached me and kneeled down hinting for me to straddle her spine. The rigidness was hard on my balls. But my soft fat pecker softened the bounces. It was short but fat. That being said, it felt rather good. I now felt as if I was making love to the *wolohan* instead of riding it. I determined that she was definitely female. We stopped, took a break, as I circled her feeling her tight ass. She was just my size. She stuck her ass out at me exposing her swollen clit. It was human...very hairy, but definitely human. I leaned forward and planted my face in her twat. Her pussy tasted so good. Was it wrong that I was engaging in bestiality? What was next, necrophilia? She loved it. She twitched and squirmed and made orgasmic moans. Very tantric behavior. *Wolohans* were made for this. That is why they were made with human genitalia. And she tasted like a sweet flower. It didn't take long for her to squirt in my mouth, filling my mouth with her delicious juice. I swallowed every drop. She wasn't done. She respected me enough to let me finish. But would she laugh at my tiny pecker? I took the chance. Besides, if done just right she wouldn't have seen it rather than feel it. I gave her all five inches. She enjoyed it. Suddenly, we came at the same time. Our cum mixed inside her lustrous, hot, and moist cavern. God, I needed that. I was so horny and hadn't nut in months.

She kneeled back down allowing me to straddle her once more. I was now numb from my orgasm. We left pleased, we were so pleased. I only hope I don't gross anyone out with this picture I painted. You must understand, *wolohans* are seductive creatures with human parts. I am not the only sucker in history to have come across this mythical beauty and fallen under her spell. If only you had seen it rather than hear it, maybe then you'd under-stand. A *wolohan* must not be compared to domestic animals. They have human souls. That's what fuels them. They get their human souls by devouring humans. Was I next on her list? I think not. Especially after the love we had just made. And as we rode deeper into the wilderness I gently stroked her mane.

We were almost there now; I could feel it in my bones. Not long now. Not long at all. So close I could see the lavish work of art. The oils were of nice complexion. The strokes magnificently pursued. It was me all right, and I was just about to grab it. Suddenly, the *wolohan* bumped me off and turned on me, breaking our lustful bond. Just as my wife did. I grabbed the painting and ran my way back through the wilderness passing the very spot where we made love. Oh, the memories.

IV: the painting

The transition was almost complete. I ever so gently placed the picture where it harkened and stood back putting it in frame. A little adjustment and…perfect. It was perfect. Everything was perfect. Life, my health, the ability to live through this wicked adventure, and my sense of well-being. Yes, God was good, indeed.

I was confused now so I asked the painting, what now?

We wait.

Wait. Waiting does so require time. Something that I don't have!

Oh, my dear Otis, soon you will. Very soon. I was growing furious now. Every damn voice was the same! A little louder, a little softer, but the same. I didn't come this far to wait. Talk to me, dammit! Now I beg of you to say something. Oh, I get it…the old silent treatment. Well, I too could play quiet mouse. No, I couldn't. I was the mouth of the South as people called me back home. My dear god, was I in conflict with myself? I mean, I often disputed the voices that shot off in my brain but never have I just flat-out argued with myself. Then the painting assured me to wait. Take a nap. Get some rest for I had a busy day ahead of me. Tomorrow would be a whole new day. A different chapter in this subtext world I am manifesting. I must do as it's told. I was feeling rather tired. In fact, I had consumed enough opium to put an adult horse to sleep. My tolerance was way beyond normal. Awe, come on. Just one more for the sake of peaceful dreaming.

If you feel as though you owe it to yourself, Otis. So be it. I can only control your thoughts. I cannot physically eradicate your ways. We all have addictions. I have mine and you have yours.

I took a refreshing quaff. Then I asked, wiping the remnants off my chin, really…what's yours, painting? Due tell. I was feeling so damn good about now. Just the mental preparedness of what's to come was enough to intoxicate with a placebo. However, the true effects were not placebo.

Haven't you figured it out by now, my dear sweet Otis? I am addicted to getting under your skin. Crawling through your veins and playing loud symphonies with your nerves.

Very well put, I thought, nice transitions of words. I patted myself on the back for my core of intelligence. Again…way too much credit.

I had to close all the windows to repent the sun's vapors. With time being lost, it messed with the solar compass as well. I nestled beneath the painting. Forty winks came suddenly for I slept for hours in this stillness of time. I dreamt that I was at home. I was so homesick, even in my slumber. I was but a child running freely through my grand pa pa's poppy field. I believe that to be when I experienced my first taste. I was ever so young and a coarse leaf slit open my lower lip as a busted bulb leaked milk into my wound. I became very sick afterward. I ran up to my grand pa pa and said excitedly, grand pa pa, it makes milk. I carried the broken stem in my hand. He was old but not too wise. Very few people knew of its properties and values. When I became sick grand pa pa nursed me in the condition that I was suffering from Scarlett fever. It was the poppy that made me sick. Even more so, the good doctor tipped his hat and suggested I take the stuff as treatment. I only became sicker as I drifted off into tiny slits of death. I believe Edgar Allan Poe once referred to sleep as this. But it was not sleep. It was a five day coma. My grand pa pa died soon; he died from a sick heart. I was young and so wet behind the ears I took it as he had a sick heart for he grieved over my passing condition. I know not that it was not so. Grand pa pa had a rheumatic heart. But that was all stitched within the fabrics of time.

My dream continued. I was now entering my adolescence. Young, studious, very handsome, and was a great workhand, as well. I was left the farm and all that came with it in my grand pa pa's will. He loved me dearly and raised me as if I was his very own. I basically went on believing he was my father, and when he died I carried a huge slice of that with me everywhere I went. Yes. Death took him away from me. I miss him more now than ever. I tell you this as part of my dream. A montage of my youth replays over and over in my mind.

I had no siblings, only two distant cousins: Artuis and Misnon. Archaic names at best. And I was only married once. Scarlett fever took my dear Jen away. She too died of a rheumatic heart. I was left in this big world alone in search of the meaning of life. Life has no answers. Just more questions. Questions that I often ask myself—hitherto. Nowadays I'm satisfied just to see a pickle on my plate. I love pickles. My grand pa pa often scolded me for drinking the juice out of his canned pickled vegetables. Scolded was a poor term. He did have a gentle hand. Even in discipline, he was overly kind.

Time still stood still. What would have been the hours of morning came short. Dreams are like full length movies that project in your mind. You can only sleep thirty minutes and dream a two-hour compressed film. I had no way of knowing what time it was. This was beginning to wear me thin. The painting greeted me by saying, good morning, Otis. I chuckled heavily. Morning, night, evening, dusk, dawn, twilight, who knows what time it is! He didn't find my humor at all candid. Well, folks back home did. Which reminded me, where is my damn watch, painting? He had it. I knew he did.

I felt these things in my bones. But he reminded me, I had one task left. Now…then on with the show. C'mon…let's do this!

They're on their way now, Otis.

Who? Who is on their way?

The painting choked back a laugh. Oh yes…my friend, you'll soon see…my dear sweet Otis.

My voice, my thoughts, why is it that I don't know what you know?

I wasn't designed that way, my dear—

Piss, will you quit calling me that. Otis, my name is Otis! I was hoping I made myself loud and clear. Loud, but not clear. The painting had now taken over my personality, which left me with a new challenge. Getting that voice back in my head. Oh, the irony. Never thought I'd hear myself say that. I liked it much better when the voice was in the statue. At least then it didn't defy me! At least then it didn't reckon me mad. At this very point, however, I had no place to go, no time to do it in, and I guess you could say on my side. I had to somehow ploy that painting into returning my voice. But without the guidance of my voice, I was useless. These mountains, this wilderness, a vengeful *wolohan* on the loose that hungers for my blood. Indeed, I was screwed.

I had to think fast before time ran out. Oh, piss…there I go again, acting as if time is a matter. Why, I had all the time in the world. That's right—I was consumed by optimism. I could go anywhere, do anything, and not reap the percussions. A person could get rather used to this life. Then why was I in such a hurry to get back? I could live forever. No death. No losses. But wait…I'd have the biggest loss of all. My friends. I had many friends back home. Why, Bill Taylor, George Watts, Benny Barker. These were only to name a few. Then so be it. I was needed at home. I already had a life there. People I love, people who love me, the ones filled with hate. That's another reason to stay. Weighing out my pros and cons my scale tipped in favor of pros. Pros meaning I leave this twilight zone of a commune.

V: hunt or be hunted

I was high up in a tree. Why?—you ask. That damn *wolohan*, that's why. She barked, howled, growled, snarled, and showed me her pussy. Indeed, I was at six and sevens…now more than ever. It didn't matter for I learned not to trust her. She had done worn out that welcome mat. It never occurred to me how long I would be staying here. Why, I was better off protected by the virtues of the house. At least then, I felt comfy and cozy, warm and snuggly. Why, I could be dreaming right now. Anything is better than this. Crepids, what was I to do?

The whole time I had been up here, I'd been slowly working loose at a branch. The tree was, indeed, resilient, but my efforts were not taken with a grain of salt. I was much stronger than I credited myself. And if non-else failed I had my wisdom to fall back on.

Moving on.

My dad told me once, before he died, that he was once haunted by a *Martua*. It was after my mother passed away when he started seeing the strange goings-on. I'm telling you this now because I often miss my beloved Jen. She was as soft as an autumn breeze and her kisses were like candy on the lips. Like Absinthe, I drank her in…every drop. And she was so intoxicating. My paranoia was like a thick vapor luring it in. I felt her drawing near. She was always drawing near. But with my vulnerability running high I had to be careful not to be tricked by the *Martua*. I said into the wind with confidence, not a problem. I know Jen's ghost very well.

The soft winds blew and rustled through the leafloss branches. I held on tight for fear of falling into the hungry mouth of the *wolohan* that skulked beneath me.

Now, I know what you may be saying to yourself. You can't pull a hat-trick in writing. I wanted to only touch base on this subject matter because it was a thought occurring in my empty brain. After all, that's what this is— a record of my thoughts. And if I live through this, I will eventually die of loneliness. The *Martua* is a very smart one, indeed…and loves to play tricks on the helpless and defenseless. I often said with courage, it would not get me! But that wasn't the problem right now. The problem was trying to break this blasted branch…oh, there we go.

Now I felt brave. I was heavily armed. Laugh all you want but seeing is believing. I was only able to break the small end of this billy-club. Now I just needed the courage to fight off the *wolohan*. It couldn't be killed. Everyone knows that the only way to kill a *wolohan* is with a bullet coated with black titanium. I had no idea of the whereabouts of a gun, nor did I care. My only concern was canceling its dinner plans. I would spring from the tree on top of her and ride her until she became tired and weak. Then, I would get off and bludgeon her to submission. At least I could knock her unconscious. That would at least buy me the time to escape her perils. But given the circumstances, I was scared shitless. She wasn't wanting to play…maybe with my entrails as she dissected my viscera. They do tend to play with their food, or so I've been told. It didn't matter. I had just enough opium left to get me through the horrendous task. But my bottle slipped from my hand and fell on her, just right, knocking her out cold. This certainly wasn't the last time opium saved my life.

I sprung from the tree and cleared her body as she lay. Still, I had my billy-club tightly in my hand. I used it to poke at her and examine her level of consciousness. That is when I noticed a blood spring flowing from her jugular. I looked closely. My god, she had been shot. A shard of the bullet lay close by. I picked it up reviewing its element. Black titanium. But that could only mean one thing:—someone had to be close by, watching my every move. Someone...as in human, I say. Possibly a hunter...a hunter for me.

I panicked. Took to heels and ran. I wasn't going to wait around to learn firsthand the huntsmen's intentions. Keep in mind...I'm lost. The mountain region is in abundance and deep and the wilderness is tall and long. But this didn't matter. None the slightest. It was either I bury myself even deeper into the woods or I would be sleeping with the *wolohan*. These are thoughts that coursed through my feeble, empty mind. Then I remembered, I forgot the painting, dammit!!! The painting was crucial for it contained my voice and in order for it to be successfully restored it would need to be in my custody...(deep breath)...Perhaps I could hide and wait. Yes...that's the dime. The huntsmen, be it he, be it she, certainly wouldn't stay out here too long. I mean, I've only been here a time-loss day and night, and I was dying to go back home. Perhaps, dying is a bad pun.

I hid behind, what appeared to be, an old well infused with weather-beaten foliage. I looked for a comfortable position so as to not be seen, and just as I found it I heard a whimpering. Why, it appeared as if it was resonating from beyond the well. How could this be?...who could this be? And to think, this whole thing started with an independent tour of the town. (memo) I must really learn to leave well enough alone. And then the voice called to me. She knew me by name. A very petite and small voice. Perhaps a little girl. My god, there's a little child down in the dark donjon before me. She whimpered some more...cried out...and then...oh, you will mark me as mad if I continue but I must for the sake of the story (after all, my judgment has already been chosen)...she spoke my name. Quietly. In a sob. A nervous whisper like a cat's meow. I had to get a closer look. Closer. A little more. Say something, sweetie. How do you speak my name? What hap—

All went silent as black consumed me as well. I awoke on the moist ground with five spawns of Satan around me—feral children. But was I

scared? By now…yes. Would you have been? Of course not. You're probably at home on a moonlit night nestled in your favorite chair by a fireplace, a
candle as light, reading about my many misadventures. The occurrences of
one day. Remember: timeloss. Then be it. Allow me to entertain you even
more. I struggle to get my bearings, gravity wrestled with me, as I looked
around for the little girl. My head ached from the pump-knot that swelled
like an egg on my head's crown…courtesy of the butt of a gun (…) actually,
a *trapshooter*—I assumed it to be from the loud blast that still lingered in my
empty skull. Then I was hit with something else. An object that spoke,
ouch, it said.

A voice from above called upon me, there…take your silly painting
to…damn thing wouldn't shut up.

Ah yes, once more victory was mine. I picked up the painting and dusted
it off, doing my best to see. You see, without my voice, I was just as primitive as these feral children that surrounded me.

Your eyes…use your eyes, said the painting.

That's right! My eyes. I was given nightvision to guide the house. Never
thought I'd have to use it for it never got dark. I must have forgotten. My
eyes glowed like two amber jewels. I looked around me. These feral children
were just as I thought. Then the little girl appeared, looking somewhat
familiar to thine vision. She told me her name was Alice and that the evil
witch of the otherworld awaited her. She was so pretty with her curly blonde
hair, blue dress with white cut collars, and white apron. But she had no
shoes.

They ate them, she answered my painting's thoughts.

And where do we find this witch, Alice?

For now, she is in the kingdom of werewolves.

Do you know how to get there because I'd be glad to escort you to the
front gate if you do so desire, Alice?

The painting laughed so hard. You chicken, it snickered.

If I go then we all must go. Even my friends—the feral children.

Wow, what a group we would be. An insulting painting, a fairytale adven-
turer, a cloister of mad children (spawns of Satan, I call them still), and
me…a courage-lacking empty-headed dummy. I gave it little thought. After
all, maybe, just maybe, it was meant to be. And what else could go wrong?
Ah yes, being cursed by an evil witch and devoured by a pack of feral beasts.
Then be it, I said, so let it be done. I bowed my weary head hanging it lower
than it's ever been.

My friends will protect us, Otis. They are stronger than mortals give them credit to be.

But how do we get there?

There is always a portal to the otherworld. That is why I am down here. The children were imprisoned, but I entered at my own will trying to get back and free the kingdom of werewolves from the darkness that fell upon them so many centuries ago.

Just curious…how many centuries?

Five.

Of course, why did I even ask? I gingerly placed the painting onto the ground (propping it against a rock) when one of the feral children clumsily fell head first into the painting. I screamed and tried to stop him but there was no use. He was gone. Vanished. It was then our eyes met (Alice and mine). The portal was inside the painting.

And away we went…headstrong and head first!

VI: the kingdom of werewolves

Darkness, finally. I grew so tired of light. Day after day. Hour after hour. Light! A little is all we need to enjoy the day, but too much sun and the heat becomes unbearable. Now…darkness has fallen upon us. The thick, rich, beautiful, black night. But the first howl, followed by the second howl, and then the third howl came. Each a tad-bit louder than the last.

If I had known nothing of the werewolves I wouldn't have been fearing for dear life about then.

In all my years, I was taught that werewolves didn't exist. Ghosts. Vampires. Zombies. Witches. A complete monster slobberknocker. And I would like to say, this is where I drew the line…that line was drawn a long time ago. So now, in addition to me finding my watch and getting the hell out of spook town, I had to help Alice defeat witches and werewolves.

We diligently made our way through the enchanted forest of the otherworld. The painting spoke to us from the heavens—the voice of our God. Wise vocalizations filled the wind, the trees, and the earth. Serenity mixed with a master's knowledge was pouring down on us like thick and heavy droplets of rain. But the voice was mine. Yes…need I forget!!! The voice the painting had stolen from me left me with a hollow head. Again, I was so infuriated. Shards of angst ripped through my veins like an electrical current. I gnashed my teeth through a thin smile. My brow furrowed inward like demon eyes. It didn't matter, the only person that really paid me any mind was the voice, which belonged to me anyway. I decided that anger would only set me back on this new adventure.

We saw darkness not too far ahead. Vampire bats, whippoorwills, owls, frogs, wooly lemurs, *windgullies*, *wolohans*, and *juagermites* entertained the still night. It was rather musical the way they did their parts in such a…(syncopating)…manner. Melodic, in a sense. Sorta like vibes and tinks of *Angelia*. But enough with the nonsense for we were now drawing near.

Closer with every breath.

I smelled the stench of foul, rotten death *danse macabre* in the air. Horrible, yes. Revolting, indeed. But the task was far from complete.

Up ahead, I see two Imperial guardsmen, whispered Alice.

So…what do we do?—I asked inquisitively. I had to for I had no clue and was getting more and more frightened with every quiet gust. Silence is not always a good thing, I'll have you know. But with my eyes, I felt secure. Everything that surrounded me was a creature of the night. My cranial senses, stripped. My inner senses, heightened. My glowing eyes, even brighter. And that's when I saw my first werewolf. It gnashed at me through the darkness. Its mouth was huge with razor sharp canine teeth and salivation that appeared as strings of slime. I knew it was coming after me. I knew it had already set its sights on me. But the feral children, they were brave. Yes…they were brave in keeping that thing at bay. And they acted as if they feared the untamed minions of dawn's society. It was then I felt all the more grateful that I had befriended them…or they had befriended me…either way, I was grateful.

With their arched, bipedal feet bent to kill, they kept their amber glows locked tightly on us as we passed with little, if no, conflict. They were designed to kill—lethal beings that ravaged in angst for their blight. And I didn't want to be the next collarbone they picked their huge canines with— the meat they would pander to. I admit that I am not a brave soul; however, I felt brave for the moment. Perhaps it was my protection that appeased my trepidation. Besides, with all the triumphs that I have attained thus far, I was ready, willing, and able to add to the magnificent list. Why, after this day…I would be known as Otis Platt the Conqueror. Too much, I suppose.

We crept our way through the darkness filled with Satan's watchmen. Alice said, in a hush, once we get inside, the worst is yet to come.

Oh, dear lord, I thought, don't tell me that! But she was right. And I knew it all the while. Satan's dogs would be nothing compared to the feat we had yet to surpass. They were just the guards. The true maniac waited for us on the inside…the witch!

The door opened and an ominous presence greeted us. I say ominous, but that's not even the word. His complexion was a dead, cold gray. His eyes were hollow, black holes. He said, the queen has been waiting, through his long jagged fangs. His face, narrow as a bat's. We entered on the good assumption that he would guide us the rest of the way so as to avoid unpleasant conflicts with other creatures inside the skeletal coliseum. And that's just what it was:—an imperial construction of human leather and bone.

We walked through the ribcage aisle as glowing, beady eyes lit up the way and sat upon me. I trembled beneath my skin as my nerves quickened. It wasn't so much that I was afraid, but my awareness was beyond my sight. In other words, I was oblivious to the surprises that lay ahead...dormant like a fatal bacteria settling ever so elusively inside one's gut just waiting to spread. But I didn't let my guard down. Paranoia mixed with fear of the unknown made sure of that. These are senses we have, but never give credit to. Slowly, slowly, slowly we inched our way down the devil's backbone. We're almost there, Alice said.

I certainly hope so, I added with intense enunciation.

At that very moment, I could vaguely see the witch. Why, she didn't look like any witch I'd ever seen, not that I'd ever seen a real one, but in the sense that she didn't cater to my expectations. And the closer I got the more beautiful she became. Flaxen strands of silk radiance caressed the perfect outline of her well-rounded face. Her smile, what euphoria it brought with it. And her amber-glowing eyes. Perhaps she had a little bit of wolf inside her, as well.

She greeted our arrival with majesty. And then Alice asked her the question:—is amnesty in your heart at this time, Enchantress?

Enchantress?—in all my years of being exposed to the mythological world of witches and the supernatural, I have never heard of a wicked spellbinder being referred to as an enchantress. But that was just the thing. She wasn't wicked at all. Whether or not she bound spells was neither here nor there...but wicked, she was not.

Surprisingly, she agreed to an appeal of amends after her centuries-old, worldly battle and run as Witch Asabelle. And that's just what we came for. I was more than relieved to know that we achieved our mission without a grain of conflict. But still, the werewolves were frightened. After all, they were animals more than men, and animal instincts are very indefinite in nature. Pins and needles, I remained upon.

What task do you wish for in return, Enchantress? Alice continued to make a plea to the beautiful witch.

Go see the see-and-hearsay spider for further minutiae, my pretty. He will listen to your plea, grant you nobility, as well as see your way back to the path you arrived upon.

Huh, a see-and-hearsay spider…this was getting more interesting by the minute. At this point, I was even more so uncertain of what imageries lay ahead. And my default fear of arachnid creatures was corrupting my now sense of confident relaxation. My confidence was now overturned by further detonation on what to expect, in other words. But calmly, I resumed. I reminded myself that the worst was over and the witch had the say in the matter. The fact that she was sending us to the eight-legged beast to be consumed like web-rendered flies seemed irrational at the time. But then again, underneath her mesmerizing façade, the wickedness of every witch had to lay dormant inside of her…and dishonesty is a wicked scheme. It was then I put all my faith in the survival abilities of the feral children. Nevertheless, they too were centuries old and had fought their fair share of battles, I was more than certain.

As I took all my concerns with me, I now found myself before the hairy monster. Imagine a robust tarantula the size of a tractor. Yes…this is what I stood before with all eight eyes glaring fatuously into my anxious soul. Her pedipalps rubbed together like two impatient hands of a hungry marauder. Then she spoke in a delicate small voice. This soothed me. Alice, I've been expecting you for quite some time.

Alice kneeled before her and explained her conveyance: I have been confined to a single rounded wall for five centuries my wretchedness. With the help of my new friend Otis (her eight eyes still examined me), I was able to escape. I had been here sooner but, as you now know, I've been a bit held back.

What fool had encaged you? Tell me now and my army will hunt him down and penalize him for perjury. All mortals are sworn to honor the myth that keeps our otherworld in distinction, you know this, Alice. Unfortunately for him, death will be his sentence.

Alice sighed deeply and unexpectedly defended the perjurer. He meant no harm. Aside from the fact he interfered with my prophecies, the well kept me safe.

Now, the spider spat fire (but not in a literal sense). Nonsense!!! (Her voice was no longer delicate.) For protecting him you will be held for obstruction. The penalty is life as a chore woman. You're much too young,

Alice, to throw the remaining years of your youth to the castle. (The spider got a consecutive glare in all eight eyes.) Why must you protect him, dear?

It's my heart, your wretchedness. It's much too frail to exact revenge upon any living thing. You know this. (Alice bowed her head.) But if I must, I will assist you in his capture. It will mean exiting the portal and entering the salvage land.

The salvage land…that's what Alice referred to as the forest upon which I must continue my journey. With a quiet voice I spoke out, will I be needed for this? I mean, I am having a hard enough time succeeding in my own obstacles. You see, I am in search of my watch that will restore time and help me get back home.

You are free to do as you wish. Imprisoning a mortal without proper cause is a violation of the right-to-be act. Morear will show you to the portal.

Morear?—what an odd name, I thought. It was no surprise to discover she had appointed a werewolf as my guide. After all…this was the kingdom of werewolves.

VII: the river of misleading things

There was something glowing up ahead—a mystical blue effervescence that shimmered gas-like fumes as it traced. Perhaps the brilliant sun above was absorbed in its perfectibility and the result was this effect. All rationalizing aside, I was eager to discover what it was. I was drawn to it like a moth to a flame and drifted under its spell. Fabrics of what used to be time peeled its layers as I slowly approached it…a body of water…deep and wide…bluer than Heaven's sky. The glow was gone, but it still sparkled. Awe, yes, the river of misleading things, the painting said.

Why, this was no river. Rivers are murky and dense. The waters I stood before were crystal clear. It doesn't look like no river I've ever seen, I replied.

Must I remind you…you're not in Kansas anymore, my dear old chap.

A futuristic quote that I had not yet known. But here, my voice was wise and beyond its years.

I stuck out my foot and easily dipped the toe of my shoe into the wet shoreline. Everything around me morphed into the place I was most familiar with—my home. The painting now hung upon my wall and did not speak. Would not speak. No…could not speak. It's the water, I thought to

121

myself. I pulled out my foot and everything restored itself to originality. Trippy, huh?—the painting said with a chuckle.

If I submerged myself in the depths, would I drown? With the river's mind-altering effects, I could live in it forever. The emptiness of my mind rattled tiny chopped-up fragmented thoughts that the painting made better sense of. Yes, it said, but I wouldn't dare try it. It would only deter you from really making it home.

Just for an hour or two? That time alone would at least pacify me and strengthen me to continue my quest. I was trying really hard to convince my own mind, but creating a conflict was all I accomplished. The painting made very valid points, but he was talking to an empty-headed sort. And I tuned out most of his argument with passive what-ifs. For example: what if I dove in right now? What if I liked it so much that I never saw land again? What if this was more a river of deceit rather than of misleading things? What if? In the end, I talked myself out of it.

As I turned to walk away, I paused for a moment. Don't you do it, said the painting. It knew exactly what I was thinking...of course. In a single gust, I turned and splashed into the river. Unfortunately, the painting neglected to warn me of its many perils. The lower I sank, the more worse the experience became. Rather than the delighted morph I looked forward to; images of familiar things circumferenced me like a cyclone. I felt like a flushed turd, yet calm. I mean, the water stayed out of my lungs and body. This must be how a fish feels, I thought. And as I quickly hit bottom, the last flash of imagery hung in its existence as the water became a scene I was all too much familiar with—my grand pa pa's farm. Yes!—in reality, I stood heavily submerged in water, but in the pseudo-state, I was in, I was ten years old, standing before my dying grand pa pa. He was unnaturally frail, lethargic, and hollow-eyed. The blackness consumed his sight as the fever distorted his brain. Of all the moments in my life to relive, I didn't particularly consider this pacifying. It was more like disturbing. It made sense, however. This was a moment in my life where I had felt the lowest. All the goodness in life must exist at the top. Perhaps I should make my way to the shore and lie back soaking my feet. That's what I should have done, to begin with. I am so foolish at times. But wait...My god, I couldn't swim if it even meant saving my life. I never learned how. But it didn't matter, for I was saved by a black mass. Swooped up like a captured shark.

I now found myself lying on the shoreline. My eyes were a blur, everything was back to normal. Once more, I was dry as a bone. Then, I saw my savior. Just a glimpse, but that's all I needed. (A mermaid!) Why, I couldn't believe my eyes. But then again…reality abandoned me a long time ago. And I wanted to dive in after her, but that would only set me back as I was before my rescue—a poor soul encaged in his own alternate reality. But it was my alternate reality so why did it matter? With my intellect on hold, I chose to dive in. However, I was stopped by a powerful force. I fell to the ground and shook my scruples in place. A *barrier-mime*, the painting said.

What caused it?

The mermaids activated it. You weren't rescued, dear Otis. You were kicked out of their realm.

Figures. I mean…with the rate my luck was going, it only made sense. Perfect sense, at that. That being said, I turned to the painting and asked, so what now?

We wait.

Wait for what?

The vessel will be arriving shortly.

Vessel? What vessel? By now, things were really out of sorts. Perhaps it was I that was out of sorts. A little worse for wear, I admit. But still, my prize awaited me. Beyond the mystic blue and pastures afar, time ticked away. Tick, tick, tick, tick…I could hear it now. Tick, tick…oh so close, but yet so far away. Albeit time didn't exist, it was still of the essence. My essence. Waiting for me to possess it and restore its eternal fair.

The vessel reached the shoreline and I boarded the small, weather-beaten, fiberglass structure. The mainsail fully erect and catching wind like a catcher's mitt. Onward sail.

The waters were still and the breeze was calm. Why, the vessel navigated itself. The sail was so scenic and relaxing, I almost fell asleep a couple of times. It brought a natural euphoria. Not as good as with opium, of course, but close enough. From time to time I would peer into the river and watch my reflection travel as I. My face stared back at me embedded in the still, mystic blue. Again, so very relaxing. I made a quick decision that I didn't want to leave the vessel. I wanted to sail forever. Up until now, sailing brought me motion sickness which consisted of nausea and vertigo. But not this time. No…not this time, at all.

I wasn't sure of how far I was from my destination. The painting informed me that we weren't too far now. However, I was enjoying myself way too much to care. My god, I literally felt like I had died and gone to heaven. Even better…it began to rain. Heaven's tears were falling upon me. Quickly, I looked at the painting for I was concerned it would ruin and my voice would be gone forever. It spoke to me as rain washed away the paint. It said, looks like you got your wish, Otis.

Wish! What's that?

You don't feel it happening?

Crepids, the pain inside my head was like a vice cranking tightly around my brain. And then it spoke to me. The voice was no longer inside the painting. It came from within me. From within my very head. Ordinarily, I'd be disgruntled over this. Not now. I was happier than a child with a brand new toy. After all, the aches never lasted long. After a couple of minutes, I was back to enjoying the sail. I grabbed the painting and threw it overboard. My voice then scorned me: No!!! What are you doing? I simply replied, getting rid of unnecessary baggage. In the same scornful voice as before it said, you polluted the river, you fool The mermaids will soon send out an army of fish-headed mermen. I was ecstatic…what the hell are fish-headed mermen? My voice explained to me that they were the male equivalent of the mermaid, only in reverse. They are very fast and aggressive. Because they have both human lungs and fish air chambers they can survive on land and in water.

Great…now I have really screwed up. It never fails. Every time I feel that I am getting so close to retrieving my lost watch, I do some ill-minded to interfere with my quest. My voice then explained to me that they are already ahead of us. And that they will be ashore waiting for us to deploy the vessel. The penalty for polluting the mystical river is very harsh. However, the voice couldn't quite tell me what it was exactly. Did it matter? At this point, it certainly didn't. I assured myself. What a way to bring me down.

I thought long and hard about a plan that would help me in evading my capture. Any ideas?—I asked myself. The voice replied with swift intellect, we have to figure out a way to redirect the vessel. Navigate a bit to the south. The shoreline stretches across the entire river. It will set you back, but it's worth it. I agreed to give it a try. After all, I was too anxious to have a conflict with myself. Therefore, we tried a variety of things to redirect the vessel. Even if we could just give it a little nudge here and there, it would be helpful. I tried turning the mainsail. My voice told me, no good! There's no wind. Remember? My voice then suggested that I stand on the edge and bounce. That hopefully, my weight would get it to turn just enough to travel to the south-end of the shore. It sounded like a good idea. So I tried it. The only problem was, I could see the shoreline in the distance. It looked like a long thin hair stretching across the river. It wasn't long now. We were almost there.

I huffed and puffed and put forth a valiant effort to nudge the vessel over. I would take short breaks to catch my breath. My feet were getting sore and my body's energy was getting drained. But suddenly, during the fourth or fifth try—I can't remember which exactly—I could feel the boat moving over beneath my feet. I stood still now and felt it even more. The only problem now was that the mermen saw the vessel veering south and they took off in the same direction. The plan was blown. We were even closer now; neither I nor my voice could come up with a backup plan. The shoreline started to take better form. I could now make out what it actually was.

It would do me no good to panic for panic would only add to the negative energy I was already experiencing.

I felt condemned. I felt like a convicted killer walking the green mile. My executioners awaited me. I was still not quite sure of their penalty. However, I knew it wasn't good. Would they execute me? Or would they imprison me? Either way, I was facing an eternity of condemnation.

The vessel was decreasing velocity. The shoreline was within arms' reach. I was there. The only thing left to do now was to get off the vessel and give my forbearing sole to my condemners. I felt it in my bones. The end was near.

VIII: the watch and other things

Against my will, I was being taken down the Shepherd's Path (as they called it). It was here and now, I had convinced myself that all my travels, my wayward journey, were given away to a soul sacrifice. My accomplishments were foiled to the bitter end, and soon…I would be too. Drats…it wasn't s'posed to end this way.

Ralph Waldo Emerson once said: "Do not go where the path may lead, go instead where there is no path and leave a trail." Very wise words, indeed. If only I'd thought of that sooner I wouldn't be detained by a faction of smelly fish-heads. (memo: if only time was on my side, I could evade these mutants and come out above all with fish for dinner.) Fish sounds really good about now. If only my voice had been inside my head instead of a deceiving painting, I might have avoided this entire situation. I was misled to the arms of capture and I must not blame myself. Then again, I never blame myself.

Ahead in the distance, cast within the neon flickering of a robust pyre, I saw a familiar sight. A stick was impaled into the earth and a jacket was draped over the top…my jacket. About that time, I found myself standing before a small body of water—smaller than most ponds in circumference, yet wider than most creeks. I was greeted by the most beautiful torso I have ever laid mine eyes upon. I say torso for she was a mermaid and the lower, fishly, half of her was submerged in the shallow depths. Around the back-side of her waters the fires blazed, and beside the flame shone my jacket evermore. I was disoriented by confusion at what raison d'être may unfold. I went with it and subsided to her greeting for it was obvious by her exquisite jewels adorning her full-bodied bosom that she was sovereign. What brings me here, your majesty?—I softly spoke.

She answered: call me Abigail, Otis.

I wasn't a bit surprised that she knew my name. I was drawn to believe with all that happened thus far that this world was designed for me and my _parapagoda_. And even more so, convinced that my death lay in the rapture. I say that because death would be a blessing right now as I faced my jury and prosecutor. It is true, I would have much rather given life in death over a lifelong incarceration. And, inside my heart, to my god, I prayed. So, I asked her again, referring to her now as Abigail: what brings me here, Abigail?

She looked over at my jacket and said, I have something that belongs to you. Something of greater power than you could have ever imagined.

My jacket?

Yes.

I went back for it but I—

You didn't look hard enough.

I lost my way. This place is like a bad dream! A nightmare!

It would not have been had you taken your jacket for granted.

What do you mean?

She called to one of the guardsmen, calling him Eye, and told him to fetch my jacket. And so I stood up, brushing off my knees. She continued by saying, take it to him. He did just that. I reached out my trembling hands and took hold of my jacket. Instantly, I felt a bit of weight in one of the pockets. I went to retrieve the item when she said: it's what you've been searching for this whole time. How very true. From within the pocket, I pulled out my watch.

Then you are only trying to help me, I said with a shaky voice.

Yes. You were hard to find, but when I set sights on you I knew you were the one, she answered.

It was you in the river!

Yes, Otis. You are correct.

Suddenly, Alice came forth, then the snake with two heads, the model, and then the lights came on inside the house revealing its presence across the water. What about the painting?—I asked.

Tom Foolery is his name. He was sent to deceive you, but I had him destroyed, she answered.

It was all beginning to make sense…sorta. I mean, they all did try to lead me down the right path. But the painting…the painting misled me the entire way. Drats…I was fooled by a piece of fine art! Alice didn't stay long. She had to return to the otherworld to carry out her retribution. It was good seeing her, however.

I asked the queen mermaid what was to come of me next. She told me that her guardsmen would return me across the river. And that when I get back I am to put on the watch, close my eyes tightly shut, and say the following rhyme:

> With time on my side,
> I must be well on my way.
> Tomorrow will bring
> The dawn of a new day.

And so I, accompanied by the fish mutants, was taken back to the river and placed on the vessel. It was then I set sail in hopes that I would soon return home. With both fingers crossed, I said a new prayer to my god, a more positive prayer, for my god is a great god that answers many prayers. In fact, the prayer I said earlier wasn't to die but to be given redemption. I would have prayed earlier but up until the moment I was faced with tyranny, I was self-convinced that my god didn't exist in this world, therefore, wouldn't have heard me even if I tried. And for that, I requested forgiveness.

… My god is splendor. …

… My god is also a forgiving god.

The river sustained its mystical ambiance. Again, I felt the same euphoria as I did before. I assured myself that I would be traveling the same distance as that from which I came. Only this time, fool-heartedness would not restrain me. I refrained myself from looking into the waters for this reason. There was just something hypnotic about that river. I didn't want to take my chances. Therefore, I focused on the horizon dead-ahead. Not only was the land my destination but it was my solitude, as well. Make it or break it, I always say. And if it's not broken don't fix it! I was the first person to have ever said those words. I don't tell too many people because not too many people believe my gibberish. It's a bit off topic, I know, but I said it at a cocktail party once, and the next thing I knew the whole town was saying it.

Anyway…the mainsail really caught wind this time as it shifted the sail. The vessel was moving much faster than before. Now, with time on my side, everything seemed to be headed in the right direction. The sun started to set, dimming the horizon. I let out a great sigh of relief. I looked at my watch and the time was 6:00 PM. It was comforting and reassuring to know that time was, once again, on my side. I then became focused on the watch. My thoughts were: I can't wait to wrap it around my wrist, once more. Suddenly, I felt a light jerk. The vessel was docked. I never thought I'd be happy to see the same place I was so happy to leave during my tributary journey. And so I departed the vessel and took a deep breath. I breathed in the calm evening air. My quest was now over and within minutes I'd be home. My wonderful home is filled with people I love: friends, family…I was almost there.

I slapped the watch around my wrist and closed my eyes. As I was told to do so, I said the rhyme:

> With time on my side,
> I must be well on my way.
> Tomorrow will bring
> The dawn of a new day.

I felt a change in atmosphere and a sensation that I had been lifted from the earth and spun into a warp. When all became calm, I opened my eyes. I was home! Excitedly, I felt the smooth lavender of my couch, I got down on all fours and kissed my coarse carpet, and I even ran to a wall and placed my hands and cheek upon it giving a warm embrace. It was almost as if the wall hugged me back. Suddenly, I subsided into a dark abyss. I opened my eyes later and realized that I had a blackout. I was now staring at four padded walls as I tussled about wrapped in a straitjacket. Vertigo swam around in my head as I felt nauseous and ill. I was now confused more than ever. Where was I? What have I done? These were unanswered questions I asked myself.

As my rage became futile, I collapsed rendering myself unconscious. The voice in my head, again, spoke to me. Solace. It consoled me as it enlightened me of my condition. I was dead.

Postface

Written by J.L. Bosworth, Esq., III
December 12, 1975
3:00 p.m., Central Time

This morning I was given shock therapy for my personality disorder. Sonsabitches zapped me back to reality. If I show progress within the week I had been assured by the administrator that I will be released. Keeping both fingers crossed. It's been going on eight hours since my last round of therapy and so far so good. I've been tested by the state counselor and things are looking positive. However, my memory is vague. I was told this is completely normal. I went back and read this very manuscript. I was surprised to learn of my previous element through my fiction.

I stated in the preface that I was a writer…FALSE!!! before my condition developed I was actually a grief counselor at the Nesbit Health Center. The psychologist here believes that my insanity began due to my experiments with mind-altering chemicals. An overdose seems to be my last true memory. I've had only three flashbacks this afternoon and, again, I was told it was normal. I remember only very little of my journey through psychosis. However, my alter egos are not included in my flashbacks, or memories.

I read on and finished the story. My imagination must have been possessed by the devil's ink. I never, in my forty years of living, knew a fellow by the name of Otis Platt.

I wanted to wrap things up with this postface to clear things up. And not a single word of this will be made public or published by any means. I have made the decision to insert this as an entry in my private journal. I now find myself questioning the reason behind my storytelling. It's never been like me to conjure delusions. But then again…never thought I'd find myself sitting in a padded room either.

I feel as though I said too much. Therefore, I think I'll wrap things up. I have been assigned to a new adventure. Before I leave, however, I have one stop to make. I must visit the grave of a dear friend of mine that had just recently passed away. His name is J.L. Bosworth, Esq., III. We've shared much excitement together and even contributed to one another to end the war. I feel as though there's not much left to hide. I mean, most of my darkest secrets have been revealed. Therefore, I must make a confession. I murdered J.L Bosworth, Esq., III with my guilty blood-stained hands. It wasn't easy choking the life out of someone with great strength such as his.

I just wonder if I'll ever be the same. Oh well, if not, it's been one helluva ride.

P.S. Bosworth owes me his life.

Signed,
Otis Platt

Glossary of Nonexistent Terms

Slapwitted: refer to yourself as dumb by means of poor self-worth
Trapshooter: particular brand of gun in the 1800s
HeadShop: a little shop that discreetly sells drug paraphernalia and other illegal items
Sopwith: a road less traveled
Boscow stars: a row of stars in the fourth galaxy
Rigamaroo: nonsense
Tink: short for tincture
Windgullies: mythical bird-like human creature
Wolohan: a type of mythical creature: part deer, part tiger, part wolf, with human genitalia
Crepids: good heavens, in other words
Martua: female ghost that represents loneliness
Juagermites: part tarantula, and part scorpion. They hiss loudly and cry out
Angelia: an overwhelming feeling of zen
Danse macabre: dance of the dead
Barrier-mime: an invisible wall that is impenetrable
Parapagoda: a sense of high aspirations

Disturbance

Inspired by true events

It was toward the end of November 1986, in the sleepy little town of Pepperell, Massachusetts. Annie Anderson started talking to a boy that contacted her claiming to live in the same town but went to a different school. "Describe yourself," she said.

"My name is Daniel LaForge. I'm tall, athletic, very handsome, and I have blond hair."

"You sound very interesting."

"So, do you wanna meet?"

"Sure. We'll go out for ice cream tomorrow after school."

"Sounds great. Where do I pick you up?"

Annie gave out her address and hung up the phone to tend to her chores. She was very excited.

The next day, Annie and Daniel engaged on their date. However, Annie seemed distracted and bothered by something. Daniel appeared nothing like his description. Instead, he was short, lanky, and had brown hair. It wasn't long before Annie made up an excuse to go home.

Later that evening, Annie explained to her sister, Jessica, that Daniel had lied to her about his description. "I never plan on seeing him ever again," Annie said. "Once a liar always a liar."

A month prior to the current events Annie and Jessica's mother had passed away due to cancer. Annie and Jessica loved their mother dearly, and constantly expressed how much they missed her. They would go to any extent to get her back.

By now Annie had forgotten all about her encounter with Daniel. It was late in the evening and Annie and Jessica had a serious discussion while watching TV. "I wish mommy was here. I miss her so bad," cried Jessica.

"Me too," Annie sorrowfully agreed. Suddenly, Annie got an idea. "Maybe we can get her back."

"How? What do you mean, Annie?"

"Let's have a séance. Down in the basement. Come on. It'll be great. We have white candles and I have a crystal necklace mom gave me, just before she passed away, in our room. We can use it to contact her."

"I don't know, Annie. Maybe we shouldn't." It was obvious that Jessica felt uncomfortable about the idea. However, Annie was able to talk her into it.

They were over mid-way through the séance when their father, Brian, interrupted telling them it was time to get ready for bed. From the lit candles and crystal necklace that lay on the floor, Brian knew what his daughters were up to. However, he considered it to be silly kid stuff and gave no more thought to it.

That night, as Annie and Jessica lay in bed, they started to hear strange knocks coming from inside the bedroom wall. "What's happening?' cried out Jessica in fear.

"It's mom, Jessica. We brought her back."

"Why is she trying to scare us?'"

"She's not. She's trying to tell us she's here."

The knocking faded, entering different parts of the house, as Annie and Jessica followed it. Before long they found themselves in the basement. The knocking stopped. They looked around when they saw a message written on the wall, which appeared to be written in blood. It read: "I'm in your room come find me." At this time the girls thought they may have contacted a demon rather than their mother. Frightened by all of this they hurried back up the stairs and told their father. "Dad, this is real. Jessica and I had a séance and must have pulled out a demon instead of mom," Annie rambled.

"That's ridiculous, Annie. There are no such things as ghosts and demons," Brian retorted. However, he went to check it out anyway thinking an intruder may have done it.

After seeing the message Brian phoned the police. It wasn't long before a cop showed up. The cop examined the message and concluded that it was ketchup and not blood. This infuriated Brian. Now his daughters have gone so far as to make it look like strange things were happening. "This is unacceptable behavior, girls. It stops now! You hear me?" Brian lectured.

The rest of the year the disturbances ceased. Brian was pleased to know the girls had stopped their shenanigans and resumed normal living.

It was now the middle of January 1987. Brian Anderson had left. However, Annie and Jessica were still at home. It had now been a month since the last disturbance. Contentedly Annie and Jessica sat in the front room with the light dimmed watching TV. Suddenly, they heard a loud pounding inside the house. Annie muted the TV and listened closely. Jessica stayed close to Annie. The pounding continued. Pictures fell from the wall. "I'm scared, Annie," cried Jessica.

"Let's go," said Annie as she and Jessica took off out the front door.

"Where are we going?"

"Next door. We'll stay there till Dad gets home."

It wasn't long after that Brian pulled into the driveway. Annie, Jessica, and a neighbor stood in the front yard waiting. The neighbor approached Brian as he got out of his car. "What is it?" asked Brian concernedly.

"It's your girls. They're scared to go home. They said something was going on inside. Thought you should check it out," answered the neighbor.

Boldly Brian went inside. The first thing he noticed was that the house appeared to be ransacked. Also, the TV was full blast and playing white noise. He slowly crept up the stairs when he saw another message that read: "I'm back come find me if you can." Like the last one, it appeared to be written in blood. However, by now, Brian knew that it was ketchup. He shook it off and continued up the stairs. He entered the girls' bedroom. Instantly he set his sights upon a third message. This one read: "Marry me." By now Brian was at six and sevens. But things only got worse. Standing before the vanity looking into the mirror was a blonde-headed female wearing a wedding gown. Brian noticed the gown immediately. It belonged to his deceased wife. "Sweetie," said Brian softly with a tremble to his voice, "is that you?" Slowly the entity turned its head while looking Brian dead in the eyes. It was a teenage boy wearing a blonde wig, Brian's deceased wife's wedding gown, and brandishing an axe. His face was covered with war paint—pale white with black around the eyes. The boy removed the wig as he took a step toward Brian. "Holy fucking shit," said Brian as he took off down the stairs and out the front door. He phoned the police and before long they arrived.

It was the same cop as before with a few different ones. They did a thorough search of the house noticing that, obviously, something had taken place. However, they found no one.

Just when they were about to wrap things up one of the cops noticed a small door in the wall with a dresser barricading it. The cop pulled the dresser away from the wall. It was a crawlspace. The door was slightly open as the cop saw an arm. "Come out with your hands up! Come out and show yourself right now!" the cop ordered. The boy stepped out from hiding. It was Daniel LaForge. Apparently he had been living inside the Andersons' walls the whole time while, in a sense, holding them hostage, but never to be seen.

Daniel was arrested with a bond set at $10,000.00. Before long he was released after his mother posted the bond. He returned home with his mother. Out of common courtesy, the cops felt the need to contact Brian Anderson and tell him that Daniel was released. This only worried Brian more. Therefore, he decided to make arrangements to move. He and his daughters felt unsafe knowing that Daniel LaForge was back out on the streets.

On December 1, 1987, in a rural Massachusetts town called Townsend, Andrew Matheson returned home after being gone for a month. He made a startling discovery. His wife and kids had been brutally murdered. His wife, Priscilla, was found nude and sprawled out on her bed. His kids, Abigail (age 8) and William (age 5) were found dead in their room. During an investigation, the police noticed something familiar about the crime scene. It reminded them of the Andersons' incident in Pepperell. Because of this, they decided to pay Daniel LaForge a visit. While talking to his mother at the front door of her house they noticed Daniel running through the woods. They looked for him but had no luck. A week later, a tipster called the police and said someone was fitting LaForge's description hiding in a nearby scrap yard. They went to check it out and found LaForge inside a storage building. LaForge confessed to the murders stating that he only went there to rob them when they returned home earlier than he expected. He, then, stated that he had no choice but to kill them. He was, thereby, convicted of a triple homicide and sentenced to multiple life sentences for the murders. The crime is widely considered to be one of the most heinous crimes that were ever committed in the state of Massachusetts. Although experts claim that Mrs. Matheson was also raped, LaForge did not receive any charges for sexual crimes.

The Culling of Wayward Inn

Mike, Samantha, Steve, Hayley, and Roger were trucking along enjoying their road trip—a three day rave featuring celebrity Deejay Cooper Malone, as well as live performances by the pick of the litter of local bands. "I'm gonna get so blitzed,' said Mike as he sat at the wheel.

"Not if I beat you first," retorted Roger. The girls just rolled their eyes impassively.

Roger was the only single one in the group. Samantha was with Mike, and Hayley was with Steve.

As they traveled down a back road, Roger complained about not being able to make it on time while arguing, "You should have taken the highway."

Mike replied, "Dude, we have over a gram of pot in the hatch. Wouldn't be wise. Besides, Katie has never led me astray yet." Katie was a reference to his GPS.

Samantha looked at Mike playfully and said, "You sure the weed will last three days?"

"Not if I can help it," chimed in Roger.

Steve began to tell an old urban legend despite the road they were on. Whether or not it was an actual story or just some fabrication that loomed from his prolific imagination was debatable. However, his stories were always attention-grabbing so the group listened in stillness. "It was 1985 when it all began. A young couple was cruising down *this* very road. Suddenly, out of the pitch black vicinity, appeared a little girl. They stopped and asked her where she was headed. Tears gushed from her eyes. 'I'm lost and can't find my way home,' she cried. 'Well, get in. We'll get you there," the driver replied. She climbed into the back seat and told them it was straight down the road."

Roger appeared stooped. "Wait. If she was lost then how did she know her house was down the road?" He did make a valid point.

Steve replied, "Okay, a minor hole in the story, but pay attention to what happened next."

Again, a hush fell upon the group.

"After traveling down *this* very road a couple of miles, they saw a two story house with a white picket fence. 'That's it!' she exclaimed. They pulled into the driveway and got out of the car. They entered the white picket fence and headed for the door. The guy knocked. After a few seconds, an even younger couple answered the door. 'Sorry to disturb you this late at night but we picked up your daughter a ways down the road. She was lost and afraid,' the guy said. 'It can't be,' said the girl's father. 'She died a year ago.' As chills ran down their spine they turned to the little girl and she was gone. To this very day, travelers continue to do the same. It got so bad that they had to put a sign in their yard stating that their daughter died in 1984. But that doesn't stop people from knocking on their door."

"Dude, that was the best one you've ever told," complimented Mike.

"And where is this house?" asked Hayley.

"Oh, it's down there. You'll soon see."

They continued their trip as Roger rolled a fat joint and sparked it. They passed it around. After a couple of rounds, a little girl emerged from the darkness. Mike slammed on the brakes as Hayley said, "Creepy."

Samantha rolled down her window and asked the girl what was wrong.

"I'm a long way from home. I'm scared. Can you take me there?"

"Sure. Get in," replied Samantha.

The rest of the group detested the idea; however, she did so anyways. She sat up front with Mike and Samantha for the back seat was full—a three-seater.

Albeit the matter at hand had an eerie similarity to the story Steve had told, Mike continued to drive.

A couple of miles down the road they approached an old, seedy motel off to the right. "That's it! That's where I live!" shouted the little girl, excitedly. A weathered sign read: WAYWARD INN—such an eerie name for the cause. They pulled into the parking lot and exited the car. Together, they entered the motel. As they approached the registration desk the girl's mother came out of nowhere and grabbed her while asking, "What are you doing with our daughter?"

The group sighed in relief that she wasn't a ghost.

"Well, answer her," said her father as he emerged from a dark corner.

Samantha gave way an explanation as the mother shook her daughter saying, "Dammit, Kayla! I told you to only play outside."

Kayla's excuse for being so far away from home was that she was chasing a rabbit. The mother, then, put her down and told her to go to her room and stay there. Sadly, she ran up the stairs.

Mike said, "Well, we better be on our way," as the group exited the motel. Right away Mike noticed that his driver's side tire was flat. He cussed a bit and told Roger to fetch the spare.

"Uhm, there is no spare."

"What? I know there is. I put it there myself."

"I had to take it out to make room for my stuff."

This made Mike even madder.

With no other option, they reentered the motel. Hayley tried to call someone for help but she had no signal on her cell phone. The others looked at theirs—again, no signal.

Mike asked if he could use the phone.

"Don't work," said Kayla's father.

They convened quietly as they came to the decision that they had no choice but to spend the night.

"Are there any vacancies?" asked Hayley.

"Sure, pick a room. Free of charge. The least we can do for bringing our little girl home," replied Mike.

The group settled on 9-B as the generous host tossed Mike the keys. "Just around the corner."

"Thanks," said Mike as they exited the motel and went to their room.

Upon entering the room they noticed a strong musty odor. "This room fucking reeks, man," said Mike.

"No doubt," agreed Roger.

Steve flicked the switch as the two girls entered last. "There's mildew in here," pointed out Samantha.

Mike came to a sudden halt as a loose board creaked beneath his feet. "No wonder no one stays here," he said.

Steve agreed by saying, "No shit. This place is a rat hole."

Suddenly, something thumped up against the window. However, it did not break. They ventured outside as Mike led the way. A dead raven lay lifeless on the ground beneath the window. "What the—?" said Roger.

"Let's go back inside," ruled Mike. They didn't hesitate.

Steve sat staring at the wall. Something grabbed his attention. It intrigued him to the point of inspection. It was a loose piece of wallpaper. Strangely, the wallpaper was the only thing that appeared clean in the room. Perhaps it was freshly put up. He pulled it back and noticed a short message. It read: *Derek Malone was here September 5, 1995.* "Why does that name sound familiar?"

Suddenly, Mike called Steve's name pulling his attention away from the wall. He had removed the loose board and discovered a photograph of a young, studious-looking fellow. He showed it to Steve.

"That's it!" Steve exclaimed. "That's the dude that went missing a year ago. Derek Malone. I remember reading it in the paper."

"You read?" asked Hayley, amusingly.

He didn't respond. He was too focused on the matter at hand—the two coincidences he and Mike had just discovered.

Roger said, "Weird."

"So what. A kid went missing," said Samantha.

Steve looked at her with an intent gleam. He pointed at the wall. "That's the exact date he went missing. A chill went down her spine. Now she understood. She understood the very reason for his and Mike's interest in the findings.

"Something's not right with this place. It has a dark aura to it," said Hayley.

Steve said, "Babe, don't start with your paranormal visions."

Suddenly, there was a knock on the door. Mistrustfully, Samantha answered. It was Kayla's father. "I thought you could use some extra towels," he said as he held up a few.

Mike asked him, "When was the last person to stay here?"

"I dunno. A week ago. Maybe two. Here, take the towels. You'll need them," Kayla's father said as he handed them to Samantha. She took them but locked eyes with him as she did. There was something ominous about him. However, she couldn't pinpoint it at that very moment. Everyone's focus was on the door as it slowly shut. Samantha slowly turned to look at the others when she noticed Kayla standing in the corner. Surprised, she asked, "How did you get in here?"

"There's a secret door in the bathroom. I put it there myself. Come, I'll show you." Everyone followed her to the bathroom. Kayla pulled back a broken panel in the wall. It went straight through the room.

"That's an invasion of privacy. Why would you do that?" Samantha asked.

No one ever stays here. I use this room to hide from *them*," replied Kayla.

"*Them*? Who's *them*? Your parents?" questioned Mike.

"No. I can't tell you. They'll take me if I do. You'll just hafta find out for yourself. They'll come. They always do." As quickly as she entered, she was gone. She left everyone mind boggled—bewildered beyond mystery.

"What the hell?" said Roger.

"I think we should leave," spoke out Hayley.

"And how do you suppose we do that? The fuckin' tire's flat and dumbass over there took out the spare," Mike said as he pointed at Roger.

All of a sudden, the room began to shake. Mold crawled its way across the walls like varicose veins. A loud and painful cry resonated from outside and got louder as it entered the room.

141

The story ends here. It is believed that those who enter the Wayward Inn are marked for death. Souls are collected and the bodies disappear from all existence. Then again, that's just another urban legend. I'll leave it up to you, however, to determine whether the cause and effect are, indeed, factual. Truth be told, Mike, Samantha, Steve, Hayley, and Roger haven't been seen since they left for their trip. Still, today, their disappearance remains a mystery.

Tangled Yarns

The following are ten of the shortest, yet creepiest, horror stories you'll ever read.

I: My Son's Bed

I entered my son's bedroom one night and found him curled up and shivering with fear on the bed. I asked him, "Son, what's wrong?"

He replied, "Someone is under my bed."

Intrigued, I looked. I was shocked to see, again, my son curled up and shivering with fear. He said, "Dad, someone is on my bed."

II: Mirror in the Room

I woke up in a very stuffy room. I was disoriented and beside myself at what had awoken me, startling me from my slumber—slow, continuous knocks upon, what sounded like, glass. I searched the room high and low. There wasn't a window in sight. However, there was a mirror. The knocks began again, only his time...louder. And sure enough, they came from the mirror.

III: The Little Girl

I was driving down a dark beaten path one weary night. Ahead in the distance, with my headlights reflecting off her little, white dress, I saw a little girl. I slowed down my truck and steadily approached her. I pulled beside her and stopped. I asked her, "Where ya headed?"

She replied in a soft voice, "Home." She pointed. "I live just up that hill."

"Well, hop in. I'll take you the rest of the way." She entered my truck and gave me precise directions to her house on the hill. She neglected to tell me it sat in the middle of the cemetery.

I walked her up to her house and her mom answered the door. Eerily, the girl's mom didn't seem to question why she was with me. However, the girl's mom did try her damnedest at making me sit a spell. Even the little girl told me I should strongly consider staying. I said my peace and bid farewell.

On my way to my truck, I tripped over something. My headlights glared where I landed. Fortunately, I broke my fall with my hands. But then, just s I looked up, I noticed the most chilling thing. It was a tombstone. It had my name, date of birth, as well as my date of death, which was October 1, 2016. That was just less than a week ago. In a glum trance, I stood up and entered the house. Talk about a family and friend reunion.

IV: I Live Alone

I woke up early one morning to a notification beep on my phone. It was a message from an unknown sender, with an attachment, that read: You're very pretty. I opened the attachment and it was a picture of me…sleeping. I live alone.

V: My Girlfriend

I was woken up late one night by an aggressive pounce upon my window. It was my girlfriend. In a frantic state, gasping for air with every other word, she told me she was being chased by a madman and begged for me to help her. She was murdered less than a year ago.

VI: I Heard it Too

A girl woke up
To hear her mom scream her name.
By the third or fourth scream
It didn't sound the same.
She walked down the hall
Calling out, "Where are you?"
She was pulled into a room;
"Shh, I heard it too."
The girl turned around
And was shocked to see
Her mom was now with her.
"Whose voice could that be?"
The voice got closer
With each step up the hall.
It drew closer, and closer,
As it came to a halt.
Then, as a presence
Stood outside the door,
The girl turned around
And her mom was no more.

VII: The Sound of a Baby

The sound of a baby can be a joyous thing. However, not when it's three in the morning and you live alone.

VIII: A Question Worth an Answer

I don't understand. If I never sleep, then why do I keep waking up?

IX: My Ex

I was startled out of sleep one morning by my ex-girlfriend. The knife I used to kill her was still impaled in her heart.

Billy Van

X: Lonely

I always feared dying a lonely old man. I never took the time to consider how lonely it would be after I died.

The Grave Keeper

The grave keeper wobbled with little control as he held onto a black granite tombstone that read: MAY SATAN CONFINE HIM AND TORTURE HIS SOUL. This particular tombstone was the only one of its kind throughout the entire cemetery.

Pouring the last ounce of whiskey down his throat, from a fifth that once existed, he slammed the bottle against the tombstone, shattering shrapnel everywhere, and threw the jagged remainder upon the grave. "Welp, Lou o' buddy ole pal, have a good night's rest. I'll miss ya, but after I find s'more whiskey," the grave keeper slurred as he staggered his way to his shed upon the hill, just beyond the graves. It was located in the darkest part of the cemetery where even shadows dared to near-dwell. Wheezing and hacking, he finally reached his destination. It was an old, worn out building with waterlogged firewood piled high on the side and an old rickety fence that boxed it in. There was an old outhouse in the back with a half-moon and three-star design cut into the door toward the top. On the other side of the building stood a tall oak tree with a long branch that hung down and scraped against the window when the wind would pick up.

It was a far cry from what most people would consider their home, but it didn't seem to bother the grave keeper. He knew of nothing else but to drink himself unconscious and to make sure that the dead slept, as well. The grave keeper went inside and started rummaging through an old pine box that contained a lot of useless objects. "I know that pint of whiskey's in here somewhere! I just know it!" he mumbled as he dug through the junk.

"There't is." He put the bottle up to his lips, holding it with both hands and gave it the most passionate kiss. "I'll never let you stray again, my darling," he joked as he hiccupped and stumbled over his own two feet, landing him flat on his face, and rendering him unconscious. As he lay there, the wind picked up and tiny drops of rain pounced on his rooftop while slowly leaking through crevices that traveled like spider veins throughout the entire ceiling. The old oak tree branch started to scrape upon the window, making the creepiest sound.

Suddenly, the door slammed open startling the grave keeper out of his sleep. At first, he lay still in a state of subconscious; however, as soon as he was able to understand the concept of what was happening, there was a sharp blow to his head. The grave keeper woke up, once more. This time, it was very dark and all that he could hear was the sound of the settling earth. He quickly became short of breath and felt restricted. Confined. Therefore, he panicked mercifully while feeling his location and realizing the con_finement. His space was limited. He realized that where he lay was every man's living nightmare. He beat and banged every area that surrounded him, splinting wood, which allowed the soil to seep through the cracks. This was definitely an indication that he was buried alive. He screamed frantically, "Help!!! Help!!!"

Six feet above ground, on the top layer of soil that consumed its living corpse, stood a figure. He leaned up against a black granite tombstone that read: MAY SATAN CONFINE HIM AND TORTURE HIS SOUL. While lowering his head toward the mound of packed soil he uttered, with a sarcastic grin, "You were a lousy grave keeper, anyway." He tossed a broken, jagged whiskey bottle toward the packed mound of soil, turned around, and disappeared into the darkness.

The thunder clapped so loudly it shook the earth.

The rain poured down as the grave keeper lay confused—drenched in rain. "Oh, my. It, it, it was all just a dream," he sputtered as his bottom lip quivered with a chill. As he sat up and looked around, he noticed his surroundings. Beside him was a packed mound of soil which, thereupon, rested a broken whiskey bottle. As he slowly turned, he noticed the black granite tombstone. Etched upon it was the name Lou. However, when he wiped away the smudge that obstructed the lettering that continued he read aloud the name Louis Manchuk. "Hey, that's my name," he said with a disoriented look on his face.

Blood House

John Martin and Sara Baker were due to get married within a week. They had planned this day for several months. It was going to be a very expensive and sophisticated wedding.

On that day, they decided to check out some realty. They knew they wanted to stay in Cedar Grove. The question was: *where?* They started their search first thing that morning, which quickly became noon. They were about to give up when, finally, the realtor remembered a house that just had a foreclosure; however, before they could enter it she had to call the bank for permission. This is where the story begins....

"Well, Mr. and Mrs. Martin. It is Mrs., is it?" the realtor assumed as she questioned her assumption.

"In less than a week. We're getting married in less than a week," Sara explained as she kept focus on the beautiful mural art that consumed the walls of the study. "This artwork is splendid," Sara paid compliment.

"Oh, yes. The mural. I believe this was done by Marcus Van Lotten. It's an original, ya know," the realtor explained in a language only to sell the house.

"Marcus Van Lotten? Isn't he that Scandinavian artist that died last year? Yeah. He was found in a sanctuary with a dagger made of bone through his chest." Sara blabbed as the realtor just nodded her head in agreement.

Later that day, John and Sara were given confidence that they stood a good chance at getting the house. They returned to John's mother's house where they had been staying. The realtor said that she may contact them either later that day or the next day to let them know that everything went through the bank okay. The rest of that day, they waited impatiently by the phone when suddenly…it rang. It was the realtor on the other end telling them that they got the house. John and Sara both went hysterical and started making plans immediately.

A week had already gone by:—John and Sara had just finished their vows. Sara looked beautiful in her white satin gown, and John was very handsome in his rented tux. They were both a match made in Heaven.

The reception was prepared as the two entered the lounge. It was a huge spacious room with white ceramic and laced décor everywhere. There was cake, alcohol, a hired band that only knew how to play Journey, and a lot of dancing. They made it through the night. The only thing left was the honeymoon.

While wedding plans were being made professional movers were hired to move their stuff into the house and interior designers were hired to organize their pictures and furniture. Basically, they were all set up.

This would be their first night in their new house—newlyweds to break in a new home—how romantic.

John carried Sara over the threshold proving that chivalry still existed.
They settled in and got comfortable.
John put on one of his old Air Supply albums as they both snuggled by a low-lit, crackling fire. The hearth of the fireplace was trimmed in marble and the mantle was pure marble as well.

John slowly seduced Sara with soft whispers and erotic kisses. She was very turned on and he was more than ready, as well. Just as John was carrying Sara to the master bedroom he slipped on something. It was very thick and slimy. When they hit the floor they found themselves submerged in a thick, gooey puddle of blood. John noticed that it was coming from the study. He checked on Sara to be sure that she was okay and grabbed onto a nearby banister for support.

Slowly he worked his way up the pole. Once he regained his bearings he grabbed onto Sara and carefully helped her to her feet.

Together they ventured into the study to see what it was. What they found next was unimaginable. Surrounding them was the artwork of the late Marcus Van Lotten—a beautiful mural of fine art. Oozing from the crevices was blood. The entire study was filled with blood. The paintings, then, became reality. Every detailed definition and molecule of paint became real life. John and Sara found themselves trapped in the painting. They weren't alone. Others were wandering around just like them. They all claimed to have once lived in the house.

The Painter's Gallery

I am a thriving artist emptying his soul into each little stroke—forsaken by his beautiful archetypes. They bled me. Now their future is the here to my creation.

I was heartbroken too many times that I turned to alcoholism by the young age of 27. I didn't trust love; I never wanted to feel that burning in my soul ever again. It's true—love does hurt. It seems that being a great guy (i.e. sweet, kind, and honest) isn't the niche. I know this because I pushed and pushed and pushed to supply contentment for the loves of my life but they turned to infidelity every time. Maybe if I treated them like the trash their many encounters did I would have had better luck. No! There is no luck in love.

It seems that I have been plagued by a dark force. Shadows follow me in the dark. Voices taunt me at night when I sleep. But it gets more physical than that. With many layers of intense research, I have discovered that I was a subject to demonic attacks. Every morning I would wake up with new scratches on my body—always in bleeding rows of threes. I read on the dark web that three scratches are a sign of destruction, i.e. self-infliction. I was indeed damaging my body with the amount of alcohol and pills I would consume just to mask the pain. I wasn't certain if it was the studio apartment I was living in at the time or something attached directly to me. At any rate, I could not escape its clawing clutch. I thought of suicide, but then the darkness would win. Instead, I chose to damage my body—my temple—my tabernacle—disdain the faith that God has granted me. At least then I would succumb to a slow poisoning death that I would be too fucked up to even care. It seemed to have worked for many artists.

I always asked, "How could one drink themselves to death?" Guess I was on a straight, narrow path to finding out.

I just didn't care anymore.

I hit rock bottom by this time. My writing quit selling. My love life turned upside down. I wrecked my truck. Wound up with many citations that I couldn't afford to pay. I couldn't keep up with the daily grind to hold a "normal" job. My ends just didn't meet. And, therefore, my thriving hunger for being a bestselling author quit thriving.

Out of all my failing relationships, there was one that I loved with every ounce of what I had left to give. She turned out to be a poisonous apple, however. But like an addict in the making I consumed her whole. I held out for three years, but the wheels eventually quit spinning. And, like the rest, she started showing signs of infidelity. Maybe it was me. Perhaps the much heartache I had walked into stripped me of my security. I wasn't always the jealous type. But after you've been done wrong as much as I have, the motions tend to take a tow on you. It did me, anyway. I just came to the point that I didn't care anymore. All of the talent had drained out of me.

It wasn't so much that I was pouring out as much as I was pouring in. I just wanted to make it all stop. I felt as though I was too far gone to turn the ship around. Befitting for an artist. Darkness escapes from the pages and consumes the flesh. And alas, I succumbed. Within the cheap hotel room, I boarded in all that remained was a smoking gun, an empty bottle, and the lifeless body that once detained the soul of a panhandling poet. However, the darkness grew darker. But I was free. And that is all I ever wanted.

I did not go alone. No. I took a soul with me. And she fits in perfectly. She was the canvas. Her blood was the paint. The blade was the brush. But she had it coming. They all had it coming.

156

The King's Maiden

This was the age of prophets, poets, romantics, and thespians, not to mention castles, squires, peasants, knights, and Kings and Queens. Wines were being drunk from their challises. The opium den stayed congested. Only to be consumed by the well-to-do. And people were dying of crude diseases such as the Black Death, the red death, and the yellow death, and consumption. Laudanum was easily obtained, again, by the well-to-do; however, it was a very lethal tincture made of opium latex and ethyl grain alcohol. It was intended for pain, diarrhea, coughing, as well as symptoms resulting from the yellow death. But it was abused for pleasure by the royal faction. And it was everywhere.

Love was an unforeseen force—a shadow—a trick of the light in the cast of darkness. King William was shrouded by love and its dense capacity for unknown creatures. But loneliness and doubt can break any man.

King William was a semi-barbaric king. Over his reign he had four wives—three of them were beheaded due to laws of infidelity. His fourth and current wife, Queen Victoria, was intimidated by this to the point that she felt insecure in their relationship. King William made her walk in a straight line. But he had his rights. Before he and she met at the fall banquet she sought to be very promiscuous and flirtatious to every man just like a whore. This weighed heavily on the king's mind. But love is an overpowering shadow of mixed emotions. In fact, it is the most complex emotion known to man; therefore, very persuasive.

"My dear, when I speak the words, 'I love you,' I am not speaking out of habit. I am only reminding you how special you are to me. You are my life, and I love you so," Victoria would say.

As always, the king's response was," And I crown you not only Queen but the queen of my heart."

Passion was fire and theirs was vengeance. But she had it coming. They all had it coming. Allow me to explain in greater detail.

It was 1095 A.D.—the dawn of the Crusades. Religion waged war against religion. John Lee Capisto, a baron of middle class, set traps for martyrs in hopes of ending the war; however, it would continue until 1291 and the fall of Acre. Otho de Lagery, known widely as Pope Urban II, proclaimed the First Crusade at the Council of Clermont.

Queen Victoria couldn't sleep. The image of her husband's previous wives losing their heads haunted her. She didn't want to suffer the same fate, and yet she couldn't help but wonder if she was making a mistake. Her thoughts were interrupted by a knock on her chamber door.

"Who is it?" she asked.

"It's me, your highness. Lady Mary," a voice answered from the other side.

Victoria sighed in relief. "Come in."

Lady Mary was her closest confidant and friend. She knew everything about Victoria's fears and insecurities. "What's wrong, my lady?" she asked, closing the door behind her.

"I can't stop thinking about the past," Victoria admitted. "I don't know if I'm doing the right thing by being with the king."

Lady Mary sat next to her on the bed. "You know he loves you, my lady. And you love him too. Don't let your doubts ruin your happiness."

Victoria nodded, but her doubts lingered. She couldn't shake the feeling that something bad was going to happen.

Meanwhile, King William was also struggling with his own demons. He couldn't forget the past and the women he had loved and lost. He had been a ruthless ruler, but deep down, he knew that he had made mistakes.

One day, he called for his trusted advisor, Sir Edward, and asked him a question that had been weighing on his mind.

"Sir Edward, do you believe in second chances?"

Sir Edward looked at the king with surprise. "What do you mean, your Highness?"

"I mean, do you believe that people can change? That they can redeem themselves for their past mistakes?"

Sir Edward thought for a moment. "I do, your highness. I believe that everyone deserves a chance to make amends."

The king nodded thoughtfully. "Thank you, Sir Edward. That's all I wanted to know."

As time passed, Victoria and William's love grew stronger. They learned to trust each other and let go of their pasts. They ruled together with compassion and fairness, and the kingdom flourished under their reign.

One day, while they were walking in the castle gardens, William stopped and took Victoria's hand. "My dear, I have something for you."

He reached into his pocket and pulled out a small box. Victoria opened it to find a beautiful diamond necklace.

"It's lovely, William," she said, putting it on. "Thank you."

"I wanted to give you something to show you how much I love you," he said, smiling.

Victoria looked into his eyes and saw nothing but love and sincerity. She knew then that she had made the right choice in marrying him.

As they walked hand in hand, the sun began to set behind the castle walls, casting a warm glow on the couple. It was a moment of peace and contentment, a moment they would cherish for the rest of their lives.

Timmy's Toy Box of Terror (a Parable)

As always, Timmy's mom sent him to his room. Timmy hated having to spend the whole day confined to four walls. He'd pace back and forth. Toss his old baseball and catch it. And sometimes, if he was really bored, he'd read a book. This usually put him to sleep making the day go by in forty winks.

This particular night, he was startled out of his sleep by a rumbling noise. He crawled out of bed and looked around and saw nothing. Suddenly, out of the corner of his eye, he saw his toy box shaking.

Timmy wasn't sure what to think.

He grabbed his aluminum baseball bat and slowly walked over to the disturbance. If it was a mouse, he was ready to whack it.

He waited but the rumbling ceased. He carefully set down his bat and started taking toys out. When he was down to the last toy a pair of giant hands grabbed him and pulled him into the toy box. It was way smaller than Timmy. However, he fit with no problem. In fact, too much. The toy box consumed him whole.

Timmy awoke with an aching head. Instantly, he looked around noticing his unfamiliar surroundings. "Where am I?" Timmy questioned confusedly.

Suddenly, a voice from behind answered, "You are in the land of the giants. You would be Timmy."

Timmy turned really fast. It was a dwarf smaller than him. "You're not a giant."

"Absolutely not, my dear boy."

"Then who are you?"

I am the gatekeeper. Follow me, your superior awaits."

Timmy followed the dwarf into a dark forest. He looked around examining his surroundings as he strolled along. "Wow," he said in amazement, "this place is awesome."

Suddenly, Timmy noticed that the dwarf was gone…dissipated into the dank twilight. "Hello! Where did you go? Hello! Hey, I think I'm…" Timmy's voice echoed as he received no reply.

Abruptly, he heard a cricket chirping. It wasn't just any ordinary chirp, however. It was very loud and the tone pierced Timmy's ears.

Timmy looked around when he froze in shock. About 5 feet away from him was a cricket the size of a Volkswagen, rubbing its hind legs together.

The cricket turned to Timmy and said, "My dear boy, you look as if you've seen a ghost."

Timmy couldn't believe it…a giant cricket that could talk. Things were getting stranger by the minute. He spoke with a tremble in his throat, "I-I-I've never seen a-a-a cricket that big."

"You're in for a big surprise, my friend. Hop on and I'll give you the tour." That being said, Timmy climbed up the cricket's side. The cricket did the best he could to assist him. However, it was a struggle for both of them.

Timmy fell and lost his grip many times before he actually made it to the spine of the cricket.

Into the dark shadows, they hopped. The cricket hopped. Timmy just held on for dear life praying that the ride wouldn't hurt him or, worse yet, kill him.

The moon was much bigger than Timmy had ever known it to be…and full, at that. Then again, however, everything was much larger than usual.

The cricket paused to take a break. Timmy asked it, "Am I in any danger? I mean, will the giants squash me like a bug…ahem…I mean an ant?"

"Only if you provoke them."

"How do I do that?"

"Steal from them…be mean to them in any way…disrespect them and their land…" The cricket named a series of ways the giants could be provoked.

"Steal from them, huh? Kinda like Jack and the…" Suddenly the cricket took off once more. He hopped much faster than before. "We got to make it before dawn, dear boy!"

"What…happens…at…dawn?" Timmy asked with a pause between each word. It's rather hard to speak when you're bouncing at 60 miles per hour. Timmy found this out the hard way.

In the distance, there was a great big castle. That's where they were headed, of course. But why? Out of all the land to explore why do you think the cricket chose the castle?

Inside the castle stood a gargantuan, burley man. He wore lumberjack apparel, had a scruffy beard (no mustache), had a bulbous nose, and his eyes sunk deep into his sockets. He looked very ominous, indeed.

The chamber door opened as the Cricket and Timmy rode in. "Deider, my word, who did you find this time?" It was now revealed that the cricket's name was Deider, pronounced (Dee-Dur).

He was lost, Sire. He's barely eleven years young. I couldn't leave him in the dark forest alone."

"Very well, very well, bring him to me."

It was obvious that Timmy was afraid of the monster. But was also fascinated by him and all he had seen so far. He pinched his arm in hopes to awaken from a dream. He has had many dreams before. However, never any this vivid.

Meanwhile, outside the front gate, there stood the dwarf. He greeted giants as they passed by. One, however, almost flattened him like a pancake. He

163

jumped out of the way as he screamed insults in the giants' direction. "You overgrown freaks of nature," he scorned loudly.

He stopped, nonetheless, when one stopped dead in his tracks, turned, and gleamed at him with eyes of angst. "Go on, gentlemen...carry on. Have a very nice day to all," the dwarf sugarcoated his temper to appease. Apparently, it worked. The giant turned around and resumed the path. He had some catching up to do. While staring at the dwarf, the others made it further ahead.

Back in the castle, Timmy stood before the giant as he kneeled before the little, timid guy. "What is your name, boy?" asked the giant. He stood shaking with fear and temporarily paralyzed vocal cords.

"Ahem...his name is Timmy, Sire."

The giant held up his big calloused hand at Deider and said, "Shush! If I wanted you to answer, I'd kneeled before you. Now, let the boy answer my questions."

Deider backed away slowly and zipped his lips shut.

"Now...Timmy...what brings you here?"

Still, Timmy couldn't speak.

The giant looked up at Deider and said, "Go on, Cricket. Tell me what you know."

"I am not sure what brings him here, Sire. He did not say. Although..." Deider paused.

"Go on..." the giant encouraged Deider to tell more.

"He did mention something about a toy box just outside the gate. I believe the gatekeeper knows more than I, Sire."

"Very well...send him in."

A guardsman opened the door as the little munchkin came excitedly bouncing, bouncing, bouncing through."Yay...hooray 'tis me!!!" He shouted proudly.

"Quiet down, dwarf! This isn't for recreation."

"Then what? What is it you want?"

The giant cackled and said, "It isn't what I want. It's what I need."

The dwarf looked at Timmy and said, "Oh, him… I don't know any more than *the cricket*, dear Sire. He just sorta appeared out of nowhere.

Later that night, as all slept soundly, Timmy heard someone calling his name. It sounded like his mother. In a flash, he rose up from the cot and fled out the door.

The giant heard the door creak loudly. "Seize him! Don't let him get away!" His loud, resonating voice trembled the castle and awoke the guardsmen. They looked around, confused. Plus, they were in their PJs. "What…What…What's the commotion?" asked one of the guardsmen.

This made the giant furious. When he shouted orders, he expected them to be completed. "The boy, you imbeciles!" Still, they stood. "Go get him!" screamed the giant, only this time gnashing his teeth afterward. Frightened, the guardsmen looked for their armor clothing. "You don't have time. Go! One more time and…" The guardsmen were gone.

All of the commotions woke up Deider and the dwarf. Deider came hopping in with the dwarf riding his spine. "What happened?" he asked.

"The boy took off. I believe he took the sacred amulet, as well." The giant calmly explained.

In a hurry, Deider took off hopping out the chamber door with the dwarf still on his spine. He was going very fast and hopped completely over the gate.

The giant thought they were on their way to get Timmy, too. However, they chose to protect him instead.

Timmy ran through the darkness jumping briar and dodging thorns. You'd think he'd been there forever the way he acted as if he knew his way. But that soon came to a screeching halt. Timmy fell into a giant puddle of quicksand. Granules were as big as his fist.

The guardsmen ran past. They must have not seen Timmy fighting the muck for survival.

Sadly, Timmy was consumed by the quicksand.

Timmy awoke as sunshine glared through his window. His mom shook at him, calling out, "Timmy…wake up! You'll miss the bus again!"

He was relieved to know it was all just a horrible dream.

He languidly slithered out of bed and onto the floor. He stood erect as he stretched and yawned. Then, he walked over to the closet to find himself some clothes to wear to school. However, as he passed his toy box he noticed something rather bizarre. There were large granules of sand looming out from it.

Just then, he saw something gleaming beneath his bed. He went to inspect it. He pulled out an amulet that only a giant could wear.

Timmy then realized…this was no dream.

Love with Broken Wings, a Broomstick, and a Curse

I never intended *things* to be this way—so many *things* of dark nature occurring at once. I never would have thought seven years ago that me leaving my wife—*(the mother of my three lovely children and co-investor of a thirteen year estranged correlation)*—would leave me with little to chance. I loved her with the deepest regret. An oxymoron, perhaps, but love is even much more complicated than that. *Especially the love that I currently pen.*

She broke my heart. In turn, I broke hers. However, she was left broken in more ways than one. For sake of a clearer understanding—*(no metaphors denounced)*—my beloved of just a little over one decade would be that of a witch. Yes, you read that correctly. Many would *hark!* themselves of a misspelling. A bitch, she was undoubtedly. But a witch, she was with great certainty.

When I was six, my mother read me the tale of Hansel and Gretel. It wasn't long after that I was introduced to The Wizard of Oz. There, I learned of the mean ole wicked witch of the West and, of course, the good witch. If only there was such a thing as a good witch. In my wildest dreams, be that a nightmare, I would have never imagined myself in cohorts with a lady in the thralls of black magic and unholy command.

"For the love of Christ and all his good intentions," I would often say to myself quietly…sort of a mini-prayer to shelter myself with protection…at least, I hoped. However, hope is as mythical as Yeti.

I'm going to apply a sudden transition in my storyline to paint a better picture of the days leading up to the now. This is a tricky element a writer must avoid using for the sake of confusing his audience. However, it is my story…a complicated one, at that. And so I will do as I wish to make it as descriptive and freakishly interesting as I possibly must. At this point, I would like to throw in the inquisition of one simple fact as a hook that is not falsely intended to trick anybody by any means. Not a single word of my rampant vocalizations is a work of fiction. I did, however, make very few minor changes to protect people, places, and things that desire to go unrecognized due to identity protection rights. But I will assure you with every fiber of my distorted being that the overall story is 100% fact over fiction. The only problem is I will be looked upon mad once my story hits the press. But after you are made aware of the demonic prison I have been condemned to, the judge and jury are the least of my concern. Death, I will beg mercifully to find me. Now I'm only left with one question: where do I go from here? But life takes its toll—and love… Love is the myth of this unholy nightmare turned reality, not the dark anomalies of folklore and fiction. Masters of terror beware…as the plot begins to thicken your belief will stray further away from the congregation of pixels that develop an image so real, even the most optimistic of naysayers will doubt their own tuition.

The Thing in the Room

The room was dark and reeked of rotten meat. A flashlight waved *threshingly* through the black void of existence. "Mom," a voice cried out. However, it was the voice of a grown man. No one answered. "Mother? Are you here?"

He searched high and low feeling every object in the room. Still, he found nothing. He almost convinced himself that he was the only person in the room. Then, he heard a noise. It was the movement of a presence—the shifting of objects.

"Hello," he said. "Who's there?" Nobody answered him. Yet, this time, he knew he wasn't alone. "Mother? Mother is that you?" he spoke out nervously.

This time he heard a whimper.

He turned.

A sensation crawled all over his body like an army of fire ants. Disoriented with fear he began to lose his balance. He fell, but something beneath him broke his fall. Then, the light came on.

As he lay on the ground he noticed that a decaying corpse lay beneath him. The corpse broke his fall. To make matters worse he recognized the day old mummy. It was his mother.

A chill went up and down his spine. Who else was in the room with him making the racket and who flicked the light switch?

Billy Van

He turned slowly to see as the lights went out once more, and a raging growl ravaged the darkness.

Surveillance Specter

Andrew had just started his new job as a Security Officer for the Oak Lawn Memorial Hospital.

He was stoked.

He had wanted this job his entire life.

His training and orientation took a week to complete but now he was flying solo.

He had his own office.

He was a liaison.

He did his own thing—as long as he maintained order and kept the hospital safe he was doing his job. But nothing could prepare him for what lay ahead.

Albeit he was trained for the dayshift, he was unexpectedly asked to work a nightshift—something about a co-worker who had to take off for a family emergency.

Andrew accepted.

He didn't care. Thus far he loved his job. And although it would interfere with his two days off he didn't mind. Andrew put his job before everything.

So, that night, he came to work. He was thirty minutes early. He wanted to assure the guy working the previous shift that he was present and ready to take over.

The guy told him in report, "Keep an eye on that area." He pointed at the monitor labeled MATERIALS MANAGEMENT. "Don't ask me why. All I know is it was passed down to me so I'm passing it down to you."

"Okay," Andrew replied, unconcerned.

Later that night, Andrew sat at his desk paying close attention to the monitors. Suddenly, he saw what appeared to be some movement—a flicker—a shadow. Andrew watched it closely for a moment. Suddenly, he saw the silhouette of a person. He experienced fear and anxiety but knew what he had to do.

He grabbed his flashlight and headed to the location—Materials Management.

When Andrew entered the building all was still. He didn't see anything nor did he hear anything. He walked up and down—zigzagging through each aisle. Still, he found nothing abnormal.

Nothing seemed to be out of place or bothered.

After five minutes of looking around, he headed back to his quarters.

He set his flashlight upright on his desk. And, as he sat at his desk staring at the monitor, he saw the same movement—the same silhouette stirring about.

It appeared to be sorting through boxes as if it was pilfering.

"What the hell?" Andrew said loudly.

Andrew grabbed his flashlight, once more, and headed to the building. This time he was going to be sneaky. He crept up to the building and went in with a swift motion flicking on the light. Still, all was calm.

Andrew was baffled.

Was he imagining things?

Was someone playing a cruel prank on him?

For safety's sake, he went in and did one more sweep through the aisles—pointless.

There wasn't a soul in sight.

All through the rest of the night, Andrew dealt with this—the strange entity that continued to pilfer through boxes, and at the same time messed with Andrew's mind.

He left a note for his supervisor explaining the occurrence.

The next day, he received a phone call from his work. It was his supervisor. He requested that Andrew come to see him immediately. He had something he wanted to show Andrew. Andrew immediately became concerned. He thought he was in trouble and feared losing his job. However, when he got there, he was shown something. It was something that took his breath away and made the fine hairs on his neck stand on end.

Andrew's supervisor played back the video and each time Andrew went inside the building to walk through the aisles a strange presence walked beside him. It was no one they knew. But it was the creepiest-looking man one could fathom. He almost appeared to be wearing a false face—uncanny.

The whole time Andrew was searching for a trespasser he was accompanied by the specter. And to this day no one knows who he once was. In fact, immediately after Andrew got transferred to work at another client site the specter never appeared again. At the Oak Lawn Memorial Hospital, that is.

Needless to say, the job that Andrew had always wanted revealed something he never knew—his ghostly acquaintance.

Ghosts do exist and they're amongst us all—even me and you.

Heatherly

My fiancée Heather and I used to have the most passionate sex one could ever imagine. Isn't that the way it goes? But just like time has its own plans the fire eventually fizzled into less than embers. We still hang in there. After all, I do still love her dearly. And I only hope that she loves me the same if not more.

The sex thing isn't on me. I mean, I want it all the time. It's all her—Heather. But I absolutely refuse to go unfaithful. She is, indeed, my one and only true love. And...if I ever...for some strange reason unbeknownst to me...find me even the slightest bit anointed by another's touch...I would have no choice but to rid myself of such guilt. My conscience is weak. Yes...I would have to take my own life.

We talked about counseling. She mentioned a few times discussing her *problem* with her doctor. But with such busy lifestyles, we both do well to manage our passion for one another stays simmering on the backburner. Maybe one day we'll move it to the front and crank that bad boy on high. However, until then, it's go, go, go, and "I love ya. See ya later." But then came the big surprise...

I decided to kick back and watch a movie on NetView one night. Heather was out with friends—her typical Saturday night reward. I had just fixed a bowl of popcorn and sat down on my recliner when I heard the back door slam in the kitchen. I stood back up, my popcorn tumbling from my lap and spilling onto the floor, and quietly headed over to investigate. There I stood, in the kitchen doorway. Nothing. The strange thing was, nonetheless, the door was agape. I walked over, bold and brave, and took a peek outside. Again…nothing. I closed it, making sure to lock it securely this time, and turned. But to my surprise now Heather stood in the kitchen doorway vamped all in tight black leather and lace. Her eyeliner, lips, and hair were all black. Her complexion was pale and her nails were red. It didn't matter to me. I knew what was coming next. That clever girl read into my vampire fantasy. But what was the occasion?

"Here I am. Take me," she said seductively.

"Okay," I replied wasting no time.

I slammed her into the wall planting a hungry kiss on her lips. With an unusually strong force, she turned me and bit my lip drawing blood. Which she proceeded to lick off. Now I was against the wall. But I did not care. Right now, I didn't have a care in the world. I wanted her to be forceful. I begged to be punished. For what?—no reason at all other than pure gratification.

It wasn't long before we wound up climbing our way up the stairs and fucking hard on the bed. Muscles atrophied, sweat glistened, and blood trickled down her mouth, her neck, and then the cleft of her immensely swollen breasts. She rode me raw. She had one hand on the mattress behind her and the other upon my chest embedding her red fingernails into my flesh. I couldn't hold off any longer. In one gasping breath, I let go. The magical moment. Because at the same time, so did she. She collapsed beside me as we quickly drifted off to sleep.

I was abruptly awoken by her—Heather. She asked, "What happened to you?"

"What do you mean?"

"Why is your lip bleeding and why are there scratches on your chest?"

I chuckled a bit and stopped when I realized she didn't share the laughter. "Heather. You were there. Quit fucking with me. We had the most amazing sex last night."

Before Heather could say a word one of her friends entered and said, "Whoa, sorry. Bad time?" Heather turned to her. "Well, again, sorry I passed out and you had to stay and look after the kiddos. Hope I didn't cause a problem. Love ya, sis. Tootles."

At that moment, I didn't know what to say. And I'm sure Heather didn't either. I couldn't play it off as a dream because the physical evidence was there. Either this was one of the biggest ongoing pranks she has ever played on me or I engaged in the unthinkable.

We're still together today but she has major trust issues with me and still refuses to admit to fucking me that night. In fact, it completely pisses her off every time I bring it up. I just want some closure in understanding what really happened that night. It's been three years since, and I'm still bothered by not knowing.

Lost in Dreams

Let me take you back to a time that was confusing for me—a time of frequent surrender. It goes like this:

I was only sixteen when the following events occurred—my three reoccurring bouts with dreams. It may sound surreal, surreal in terms of dreamlike. Indeed, it was. But reality endorses dreams like a rampant beast of burden. I didn't know when I entered my first reverie, my state of prolonged sleep, but I loved it. The doctors were stumped from the beginning. I experienced no trauma, mental and/or physical, whatsoever. I would just fall asleep and not wake up for weeks. And the number of labs and radiology I had done were plentiful—blood work, CT scans, MRIs, you name it.

My first account happened just so:

Butterflies—plenty of butterflies—aloof in mental state, yet alert and oriented at the beauty and awareness of their majestic presence. But there was one particular butterfly that enthralled me like no other. It was the rarest swallowtail I'd ever seen in my life. It hadn't a name—at least not to my knowledge. Its colors were like Picasso's canvas on the dreariest of days—sad, yet awe-inspiring. I chased it quite a distance. I lost my way. I came to a house. A lady stood at the window undressing—full frontal nudity. Her breasts were so robust. Her pubic hair was so well trimmed.

Then the swallowtail landed on her windowsill. I couldn't believe it. What was I to do? It didn't matter. I woke up. The dream played out slowly in my mind like a strung-out movie—kind of a slow burner. Doc was shocked when I awoke. Apparently, I'd been out for somewhat a week or so. No shocker. Happens all the time.

By now these sleep studies were getting old. I mean, we all dream. Right? But apparently, my dreams were research-worthy. I didn't understand a minute of it. No one told me anything. Not even my family.

My second account happened just so:

It was just like an old urban legend—like the man hiding under the bed with a message written on the wall reading, "Humans Lick Too." Remember that one? Well, this was a Pomeranian named Max. The dog sat at the foot of my bed, and for some unbeknownst reason, I had a nightly routine. I would pet him on the head twice, turn out the bedside lamp, and crawl into bed. Then the dripping began. I turned on my lamp and checked the kitchen faucet first. Nothing. Dry as a bone. I repeated my routine. Again, more dripping. I turned on my lamp and checked the bathroom sink. Nothing. But the dripping got louder. It was coming from behind my shower curtain. I ripped it back and Max hung swinging from the head with his blood tapping the tub. What was I petting? Didn't matter. I woke up. Again, the Doc acted shocked and so did everyone else. Another slow burner movie in my mind. But the third and last dream is the shocker. It happened just so:

I was admitted to the hospital somewhat three to four weeks ago. I filled out my questionnaire and mentioned my vivid dreams and was told by several of the staff that I was being admitted for a sleep study and dream evaluation. Now, I always thought it was against some federal law that doctors couldn't lie to you but it turned out that it was comas that I was experiencing—not dreams. My family was even in on it. Was this real or is it all just one big dream sequence?—worst yet, have I been comatose this whole time? "Oh, dear God, please let me wake up!!!"

Safe Haven Way (Condensed Version)

Inspired By True Events

> *"Don't underestimate the meek;*
> *They may turn out to be far from weak."*

—*Traditional Proverb*

In the summer of 1993, the Clark family purchased a two-story Victorian-style mansion located at Safe Haven Way, a secluded plantation near Bancroft, Kentucky. These are the accounts that occurred five years later.

The News Brief:
July 6, 1998

"Another home invasion occurred yesterday evening. Police are definite that this invasion is associated with previous occurrences. This makes the third home invasion this year with the first one occurring back in May.

"Dubbed *The Full Moon Bandits*, this *band of hoodlums* only come out every twenty-nine days during the full moon. An anonymous tip was given to police early this morning. The tipster made it clear that she was unable to make a full description. However, she did see four young men, possibly in their late teens, leaving, what she was unaware of, then, as being *the scene of the crime*. From what she saw the men appeared to be African-American in descent.

"In conjunction with the other two accounts, there is one missing person while the remaining survivors have sustained debilitating injuries, or so I am told. Details are pending as the story unfolds.

"Police are putting all their effort into apprehending the perpetrators, but for now they strongly advise everyone to invest in some sort of security system and, as always, keep the doors locked. Be aware! These individuals are armed and extremely dangerous. Trust only those you know.

"Anyone with information leading to their capture should call the number below immediately.

"Vanessa Harrington. This has been a Channel 13 news brief with our affiliate radio station WKPB. Back to you, Sam…"

The News Brief:
July 12, 1998

"It is now confirmed that last week's home invasion victims were the Steward family. Brenda Steward, wife of Michael and mother of Kelly, Madison, and Shawn remains missing while Michael and daughters Kelly and Madison have been released from the hospital with no word yet on their current condition. However, it saddens me to report that young ten-year-old Shawn is in a coma.

"You can send donations to the Steward family to show support and to help with Shawn's recovery by visiting our secure site at www.ch13wkpb.trd.

"Vanessa Harrington. This has been another Channel 13 news brief with our affiliate radio station WKPB. Back to you, Sam…"

August 4, 1998

And the sign before the drive read: Safe Haven Way.

4:00 PM—Richard stood outside his house making the last modification to his *security system*. He looked at the palm of his right hand, which appeared to be very sore. He worked his fingers to and fro, in an effort to work out the pain.

Supper smelled delicious seeping through the window so he resumed his project in an attempt to finish up. With a sore hand, progress quickly became futile.

Aside from all that, the sweltering heat was getting much too searing for him to mask. Therefore, he gathered his tools, tossed them inside his small toolbox, and entered the cool comfort of his two-story mansion. Of course, he headed straight to the kitchen.

"What's cooking, good looking?" asked Richard setting his toolbox on the countertop—the very same counter his wife, Carol, was preparing supper on.

"Oh no, you did not just do that. Put your tools up where they go, Richard. And when you're done the Mean Green is in the utility room—second shelf."

"Yes, Drill Sergeant, I'll get right on that."

Richard returned but without the Mean Green. Instead, he headed straight for the sink and commenced to washing his hands which splattered specks of grime everywhere. Carol started her bitching. "I did not take you in to raise. Get a paper towel and wipe that up." Richard dried his hands and grabbed hold of her, whilst giving her ass a squeeze. "Dammit, Richard, I'm not playing! Unhand me, you beast!"

Richard poked a joke as he rubbed his canines with both of his thumbs. "The beast in me is something you'll never get to see."

"Ain't that the truth…" Carol looked at Richard with mordancy.

"And what does that mean?"

About that time Danny, their eight-year-old son, appeared at the island with colored pencils and construction paper. "Whatcha guys talkin' about?"

"Nothing that concerns you! Draw Mommy a pretty picture." The look on Richard's face was priceless.

"He's smarter than you give him credit for. It's not like he sits in front of the TV watching Lamb Chop and Sesame Street twenty-four-seven on Netvid."

"He's my baby and will always be. Remember that, mister bad influence."

"Whatever… By the way, I'm pretty sure I fixed the breach."

"You better have. It's a full moon tonight." As Carol was talking Richard started to mess with his right hand again. "Oh, how's it looking?" She looked at it and saw that it was beginning to weep a little. "Hold on, I'll get the first aid kit." Sometimes it was like she was raising three kids instead of two. Meanwhile, Danny was in deep contentment with the picture he was drawing.

Carol returned with some gauze and tape. She wrapped it and patted Richard on his ass. "Now you're the bad influence," said Richard as they shared a brief moment of laughter.

"Now do me a huge favor."

"Anything for you, my beloved."

"Go upstairs and tell that daughter of yours to turn that damn music down!"

"But she yells at me. She's at that age, you know."

"You're telling me that you're honestly afraid of a fourteen-year-old girl."

"I'm afraid of any chick on her period." That called for a brief interlude of silence. The dead stare in Carol's eyes said it all. Therefore, Richard headed up the stairs and down the hall.

He knocked first but there was no answer. The music was much too loud. He swung the door open as his daughter stood dancing in front of the mirror in her *emo* attire, black spiked hair, and dark makeup. Richard called to her at first, "Meg!" as she continued to dance—very provocative at that. He called to her once more, "Meg!" Still, there was no response. The initiative had to be taken. As soon as the digits hit *0*, Meg snapped. Her callous tones could be heard throughout the entire house easily. It didn't take but a minute for Richard to come flying back down the stairs. And, of course, the music went back up.

"That girl is in dire need of some radical discipline."

"And you're the father. Gee, go figure."

"Hey, I can fix a lot of things but I can't fix crazy."

"Funny," Carol said as she went to the stove to tend to the food.

Richard crept up behind her and caressed her delicately. "You packed?" he asked.

"Yeah, I am. The kids are another story."

Richard looked at his palm again and said, "Just make sure Mom's security alarm is activated and working. Lock *all* doors…"

"I know, Richard. We do this every twenty-nine days, remember?"

"Just don't like the fact that I'm not going to be there to de—"

"Oh, please! You couldn't fight your way out of a wet paper sack. Trust me! Momma's got two shotguns and one rifle. The shotguns ain't hard to load and the rifle stays loaded at all times. I'm a mom with the instincts of a panther. We'll be safe."

"I'll hold you to that."

5:00 PM—Carol's uncouth demeanor triggered something inside of Richard. As it always did. Consequently, he headed straight to the brewery in the living room. He filled a tumbler with brandy and didn't waste any time taking a gulp. Carol entered. "Great, now while we're out fighting off the hoodlums you're going to be drunk as shit. My god, Richard, the last thing our town needs is a drunken beast on the loose."

"I don't plan on getting soused. Besides, once the moon hits, I ain't going anywhere."

Meg and Danny entered the room, seeing their dad with liquor and hearing them argue only led to one hypothesis: Daddy fell off the wagon…again. Abruptly, Meg asked, "Is supper ready?" Clever tension breaker.

Carol replied, "You kids get the table set and have a seat. Your father and I will be in there in just a bit," as she gave Richard a spiteful glare.

It was more like an hour with an insensitive and penetrable commotion soaring the room like rabid bats where Meg and Danny awaited patiently— *not to mention they were starving.*

6:30 PM—they all joined hands. Danny said grace (a very condensed version). Right after, Meg attacked the scalloped potatoes. Richard complained because his steak wasn't bloody enough. Danny shoved a yeast roll into his mouth and plopped his head on the table. Carol made it clear that she just wasn't hungry.

Richard said, "Look, I can fix this." He started a smooth conversation—idle chat. "So, how much more stuff do you kids have left to pack?"

Danny replied, "Got almost everything. Just my colored pencils and paper mainly."

"Meg…how about you?"

"Just got a few CDs left to grab, is all."

Dusk was slowly settling in.

Meg and Danny conversed about everything they had planned for their sleepover with "Granny Anne," as Danny called her.

With an abrupt outburst, Meg turned to her father and said with dissident teen spirit, "And while we're all having fun, you'll be left here alone going through another one of your *transformations*…" She was indeed pushing it.

It was Carol's turn to be abrupt. She slammed her hand, flat palmed so that it made a loud pop, on the table and said abrasively, "There will be enough of that, young lady"

Richard pushed his half-filled tumbler aside and said, "We agreed not to discuss that." By the expression on his face, you could tell Meg's statement struck a nerve. "You kids just need to go to Grandma's house and be safe." Richard, then, looked at his palm again and saw that blood was soaking through his dressing. He told the kids, "Go round up your things. It's about time." They didn't hesitate a minute to follow that command.

As Meg and Danny went up the stairs to get their things the Full Moon Bandits made their entrance.

There were four of them—three skinny ones and one stalwart one. They wore wolf-faced ski masks, black latex surgical gloves, and thin black coveralls with black army boots. However, they had potato sacks duct taped around their feet to hide their sole impressions—clever, to say the least. To make matters worse, they each brandished a small firearm.

The stalwart one started shouting in a frenzy, "Where are the kids? Where're the damn kids?" He, then, looked at one of his skinnier allies, referring to him as *Tipsy*, and shouted, "Go find 'em! No one's getting out of this creep show alive. Not this time."

Richard and Carol just sat frozen and didn't say a word. But the look of concern that poured over Richard's face spoke louder than words.

"Whataya want me to do, Killa? How about me?" The stalwart one's nickname was now revealed—*Killa*.

Killa looked at him, referring to him as *Prince*, and, then, Carol, and said, "Take her! And don't fuck it up this time." They locked eyes. "You know what I'm talkin' about."

Prince grabbed hold of Carol, wrestled her to the floor beating her to submission, and, then, dragged her up the stairs. Poor Richard just sat there fidgeting. With a gun pointed straight at his head, there wasn't much he could do. He just sat in good faith—the faith that they would come out of this alive. *It's almost like he knew.*

After Prince took Carol, Killa looked at the only bandit left and called him: "*Show Dawg!*" He looked up as Killa continued by saying, "Go help Tipsy with those two kids. I'll take care of," he locked eyes on Richard with a devious grin, "Daddy."

Killa whacked Richard in the jaw with the butt of his gun. "How's this for a paper sack?" said Killa which indicated to Richard that they had been outside the house watching them throughout the day. Richard turned to Killa with narrow eyes as Killa hit him again. "Don't you ever look at me! You got that, bitch?"

6:45 PM—Meg and Danny were in the living room tethered to two chairs back to back. Duct tape was over their mouths, but Danny's tape kept coming loose from all his tiny teardrops; his black eye shed the most tears. However, Tipsy sat nearby and kept applying it.

Richard was laid out in the living room floor facedown, barely conscious, choking on a pool of his own blood. He was tethered heavily with jute and had duct tape over his mouth, as well.

"C'mon, guys. Let's check this mansion out," said Killa as he took off through the house with Tipsy and Show Dawg right behind him. They ravaged everything turning a beautiful home into a pig's sty.

Killa discovered a huge antique jewelry chest at the end of the hall and ransacked through it. The other two just watched. "Don't you boys just stand there. Go get the bag. Let's load up on this shit! There's at least ten grand here—guaranteed." Tipsy and Show Dawg did as they were instructed. When they returned with the bag Killa asked them if they had seen Prince.

Tipsy shrugged his shoulders but Show Dawg answered, "Where do you think he is? He took the mom upstairs."

Prince crept up behind them still zipping his pants. "You boys talkin' about me?" All Killa could do was look at him with discontentment.

"Let's see what else these rich mothafuckas are hidin'." Again, Killa led the way.

While Tipsy, Show Dawg, and Prince continued their quest for probable fortune, Killa returned to the living room. Richard was fully conscious but still just lay there. Killa kneeled beside him and started asking him questions—questions such as: *How long have you lived here? How much money does it take to establish so much?*

With all the tape on Richard's mouth, he couldn't respond to any of the questions. Therefore, Killa removed the tape. However, Richard, still, remained silent. Killa went into an emotional rant about how he barely had a piece of ice to suck on in the summer. But all of this only made Richard more upset.

About five minutes into Killa's spill Richard interrupted him by saying, "When I break free from here, you and those cocksuckers you call friends are dead."

Killa chuckled and replied by saying, "One problem with that theory, bitch! I plan on killing you first. Then, your little kids. Then…the whore upstairs."

Richard was infuriated; however, his hands were tied—literally. Therefore, he felt the need to maintain his composure and use his mental strategy with propositioning techniques. "Set the kids free, my wife too, and do whatever you want to me. I have over five million dollars in stocks and bonds. I can sign them over to you. Just let my family go."

Again, Killa chuckled. "Why do that when I can kill all four of ya and still make with the loot?"

The full moon had replaced the sun as darkness skulked through the house like ominously wandering shadows.

8:30 PM—Richard clenched his fists in pain. Blood started to gush from the dressing. It intrigued Killa to find out what was wrong with his victim's hand. Therefore, he inadvertently unwrapped it. In the palm of Richard's hand was a five-pointed star inside a circle—a pentagram. Richard's palm gushed blood profusely and even began to bubble. Killa jumped to his feet and said, "What the f—?"

Suddenly, the house began to come alive. It expelled a noise Killa had never heard a house fabricate in all his years. In a panic, he looked around as steel bars ejected from the floor. They ejected from the ceiling, as well. The house was quickly turning into a cage—a prison cell. Windows and door-ways were becoming pinfolds. The walls were reinforced with black titanium laced with Aconitum.

Killa looked back down but Richard was no longer there—blood, duct tape, pieces of rope, a bloody bandage, and a trail of torn clothing (the clothing Richard wore) were strewed across the floor, but there was no physical sign of Richard.

Tipsy came stumbling into the room holding up a sheet of construction paper saying, "Damn, we got an artist." He looked around confusedly. Now all the rooms began to lock down. "And why the hell are we in Alcatraz?" He held the picture out to show Killa. The picture was Danny's interpretation of a hairy monster. Above his drawing the word *DADDY* was sloppily written. Killa stared at the picture in disarray. The howl of a ravenous wolf then came from within the house.

The breach. It wasn't to keep the home invaders out. It was to keep the monster in.

"Holy shit, we're trapped inside," said Killa nervously as he turned to Tipsy. "This ain't no house! This is a wolf's cage—a mothafuckin' werewolf!" He began to panic as he started gathering up their things. He shouted random orders at Tipsy. "Get the others! Help me pick up this shit! Don't just stand there! We got to go!" But still, Tipsy just stood there.

"Killa...bruthaman...there is no way out. We're sittin' ducks." Tipsy's voice was shaky—an unsettling incarnation of fear and panic—the epitome of uncertainty.

"Quack all you want. I'm gettin' while the gettin's good."

About that time a humongous dark mass rose behind Tipsy. He could feel the hot breath coming down on his neck. Slowly, he turned. Blood splattered everywhere followed by another ravenous growl.

With huge bipedal feet, the beast started toward Killa. Show Dawg attempted to assault the beast from behind but a mere attempt is all it was. Claws like steak knives, teeth like jagged glass, and eyes like two amber beacons in the night—the beast wanted Show Dawg to examine closely what he was up against just before... And just like that, it was all over.

By the time the beast turned back around Killa was nowhere in sight. The only people left in the room were the beast, Meg, and Danny. The beast took off in their direction but stopped when he heard someone trotting down the stairs. It was Prince, again, zipping his pants. He froze instantly in fear as the beast flexed his upper chest and growled fiercely in his direction. Without a second's delay, the beast lashed at him and shredded him apart effortlessly as he collapsed where he stood in subjection to his demise. When finished, the beast headed for Meg and Danny but was distracted, a second time, by a clobbering of footsteps on the second floor. All Danny could do was gush tears as he shook in fear watching his possessed and physically altered father perform unthinkable acts. Meg, on the other hand, was more intrigued by the beast's appearance and abilities. She just sat and stared at it with her father's eyes.

The beast headed up the stairs. There was one more left and the moon was still full.

Killa was balled up within a shroud of darkness. His only sense of survival was sound. He could hear creaking and heavy panting but with Carol in the next room, squirming and bouncing around, making nine kinds of racket, it was hard for Killa to dissect the source. And he was too frightened to justify the means. He felt more protected wrapped in the darkness like a security blanket. But he neglected to take into consideration one major drawback…wolves have night vision. That is why globs of hot slimy drool ran down his head and over his face.

Killa made an inept attempt to escape but the beast was too quick and agile. Razor sharp claws and teeth were all that Killa saw coming at him—snapping at him like a bad nightmare. With gridiron reflexes he took to his heels—a victorious flee. But the beast was far too determined and still hungry.

Killa headed for the stairs but the beast intercepted his escape route. The two stared deep into each other eyes but the beast's attention was distracted by a familiar voice wailing out, "Help me!"—it was Carol. She had somehow managed to work the duct tape loose from her mouth. Putting Killa on the back burner, the beast responded to the call. After all, he wasn't going anywhere.

It stood over Carol with human emotion. With a sad heart, it stared at her as she lay spread eagle and nude on the bed and bound to the posts. Its brow furrowed as a single tear trickled down its furry cheek. This wasn't the beast; it was Richard. And he reached from deep within to assure her.

Carol stared at him with a mixture of fear and conformity. She had never seen *the beast* and was uncertain of its current docility or even its capabilities.

Richard reached out to touch her with his trembling hand but what Carol felt was a huge, hairy paw; still, the touch was gentle. It was undeniably Richard's touch.

Suddenly, Killa entered the room with a gun in each hand. He was ready, willing, and able to shoot the slightest movement. However, the beast was not there. Carol still lay bound to the canopy posts but a sheet was pulled over her.

Killa walked on eggshells as he slowly approached the bed. He aimed the gun, close range, at Carol's head. She begged him not to shoot. "You took from me…I'm gonna take from you," Killa said mercilessly. But just as quick as he entered he was gone—jerked to the floor with brute force. The beast was only buying its time as it hid beneath the bed waiting to attack.

191

The beast was short of leverage as it struggled to control the *squirrelly* fuck. It was difficult for it to maintain a tight latch on its prey and emerge from the bed to complete the kill.

The bed continuously bounced with a gravitational pull of approximately ten inches at the least. That being said, Carol bounced with it—very uncomfortably—her titties rebounding from off her chest.

Again, Killa managed to escape.

Paranoia and panic, especially in the presence of consternation, is a very mind-altering combination. It didn't matter where Killa was or even how well he presumed to be hidden; the beast was in his head. And he knew his only means of survival was to wait for daylight. If he could manage to stay alive until then the beast would shift back into human form and the security system would deactivate allowing him to retreat and never look back. But Killa made one slight error in judgment: he returned to the bedroom to retrieve the guns he had left during his life-threatening bout with the beast.

As he entered the room, his head filled with eyes, he looked everywhere to be certain the beast was nowhere in sight. He grabbed a nearby nine-iron to arm himself. He used the nine-iron to lift the flounce beneath the bed to have a peek. Nothing! Abruptly, Carol started screaming for Richard. Killa sprung to her as means of shutting her up. However, before his feet even hit the ground the closet door swung open throwing him against the dresser and rendering him unconscious. The beast made a trenchant attack on all fours like a rabid dog in a chicken coop as Carol watched.

The dull morning sky was entertained by the sun as all appeared calm at Safe Haven Way.

The News Brief:
August 5, 1998

"Today, I'm standing at the exact location of a brutal massacre. Four men, who police are certain were the notorious *Full Moon Bandits*, were discovered this morning by last month's victim...Michael Steward.

"Michael, claiming to be a close friend of the Clarks, entered their home on the suspicion that something was wrong. Upon doing so the grisly remains of Dante Miller, Trayvon Scott, Demetrius Wallace, and Jazz King were discovered. The Clarks' whereabouts remain unknown at this time. When asked to speak, Michael Steward had this to say:"

"I don't know what's going on here. I've known Richard and Carol Clark for a good five years. They moved down from some suburb near New York to get away from all the violence—just after the Stein Brothers, those serial killers that were all the talk a few years back were found mutilated."

"An investigation is well underway. Stay tuned to this developing story.
"Vanessa Harrington. This has been a Channel 13 news brief with our affiliate radio station WKPB. Back to you, Sam…"

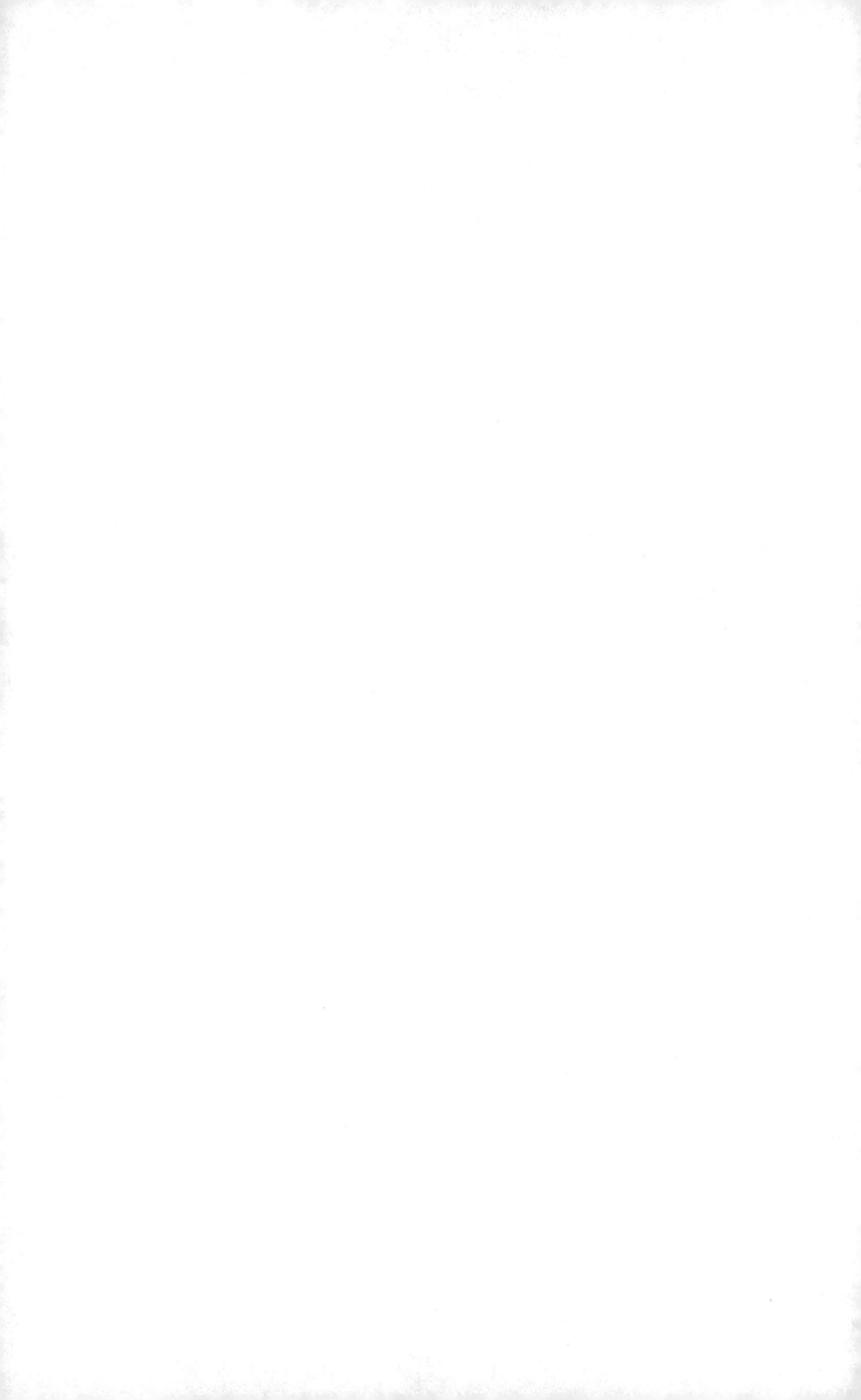

About the Author

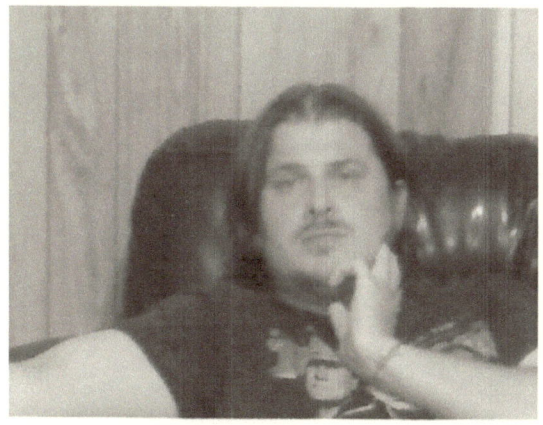

Billy Van is an accomplished author and content creator, born on December 11, 1975, in Eldorado, IL. He is best known for his thrilling works of fiction, including "The Willies" and "Whispers in the Dark".

Aside from his successful career as a writer, Billy is a devoted father to his two children and is in a happy and fulfilling relationship.

Despite facing adversity, Billy has overcome obstacles and continues to pursue his passions. In August of 2021, he was involved in a near-fatal car crash. However, through his determination and resilience, he made a full recovery and has continued to produce compelling content for his YouTube channel.

Billy Van is an inspiring individual who has shown that with hard work and perseverance, one can achieve their goals, no matter the challenges they may face along the way.

www.ingramcontent.com/pod-product-compliance
Lightning Source LLC
Chambersburg PA
CBHW032000170526
45157CB00002B/482